LET'S TALK SENSE ABOUT OUR SCHOOLS

# LET'S TALK SENSE

# ABOUT OUR SCHOOLS

*Paul Woodring*

*Professor of Psychology*
*Western Washington College of Education*

**McGRAW-HILL BOOK COMPANY, INC.**

NEW YORK     TORONTO     LONDON

LET'S TALK SENSE ABOUT OUR SCHOOLS

FOURTH PRINTING

Library of Congress Catalog Card Number: 53-9020
Published by the McGraw-Hill Book Company, Inc.
Printed in the United States of America

To
JEANNETTE

# PREFACE

This book is for parents, for teachers, and for all citizens who are interested in the public schools. Perhaps not *quite* all. It is not for those who are afraid of thoughtful criticism or for those who would avoid controversy, for the author believes with Whitehead that "a clash of doctrines is not a disaster—it is an opportunity."

This book will give little satisfaction to those who would solve our problems by having the schools return to the practices of some bygone day; neither will it please those who accept any educational practice provided only that it carries the label of "Progressive Education." The education of the future must be better and more complete than was the education of our grandfathers, but it must also be based upon clearer thinking than was the progressive education of the twenties and the thirties.

This book gives no support to those who think the three R's are the *only* fundamentals; neither does it support those who hold that all school activities are of *equal* value. The time has come for us to make some decisions as to what is important in education; these decisions must be made by all the people.

This is not a book of answers but a book for those who seek to find their own answers. It is for those who, knowing that the school of today has been greatly influenced by the philosophy of John Dewey, wish to understand Dewey but not to worship him. It is for those who believe that teaching is the most important of all professions in a democracy and who are convinced that there is need for improvement in that profession.

It is for those who can agree with the author that despite all the current debate there is no real conflict of interests between the teachers and the parents. That which appears as conflict is but the confusion which precedes decision.

## *Acknowledgments*

The theme of this book developed out of an article, "An Open Letter to Teachers," which was published in the July, 1952, issue of *Harper's Magazine*. Parts of Chapter 1 are adapted from this article.

Chapter xii is adapted from the author's article which was first published in *U.S.A.* in October, 1952, and later reprinted in a shorter form in the *Education Digest* of December, 1952. The author wishes to express his indebtedness to these magazines for their encouragement.

The author and the publisher are most grateful to the following publishers for permission to quote from the books and magazines listed:

*Life* magazine, for permission to quote from the Roper survey on education and from an article by John W. Sperry, both of which appeared in *Life's* education issue of October 16, 1950.

The Macmillan Company, for permission to quote from John Dewey's *Experience and Education* and *Democracy and Education*.

American Council on Education, for permission to quote from *Teachers for Our Times*.

To G. Lester Anderson, Dean of Administration, University of Buffalo, for permission to quote from his paper which appeared in the *Third Yearbook* of the American Association of Colleges for Teacher Education.

# CONTENTS

# LET'S TALK SENSE ABOUT OUR SCHOOLS

# CHAPTER I

# THE NATURE OF THE CONTROVERSY

Never before in our history has there been such widespread discussion of public education as today. Entire issues of popular magazines and journals of opinion have been devoted to critical examinations of the schools; each year more books are published which attack current educational practices; in meetings of boards of education and citizens committees more and more voices are raised, demanding changes.

While educators are well aware of this criticism, many have been reluctant to interpret it as a ground swell running against the new education. They have preferred to believe that *all* these attacks are motivated by malice, by a desire to reduce taxes, or by ignorance of what is actually going on in the schools. And because they have not met it fairly, the criticism has continued to grow.

If we teachers will but spend a little time with groups of thoughtful and informed citizens under circumstances in which we are not identified as educators, we will quickly learn that our assumptions as to the sources of the criticism have been, in large part, based upon wishful or ostrichlike thinking. We will find that many of the criticisms come from honest, informed citizens sincerely concerned about one or more aspects of the current educational trend. While it is true that some of the most vocal critics have been misinformed and that others have ulterior motives, the great public espousal of these criticisms rests upon a long-standing and long-suppressed feeling of vague dissatisfaction. We can quell this dissatisfaction neither by calling our critics reactionary nor by raising suspicions as to their motives. We must try to understand the true nature of the complaint and answer it fairly, conceding our mistakes where we have made mistakes.

The more honest and the better informed critics are trying to say these things:

1. The public schools in a democracy belong—or ought to belong—to the people, but professional educators have progressively preempted the responsibility for policy making to such an extent that interested citizens, even members of elected boards of education, feel that they no longer have an adequate part in the establishment of basic educational policies.
2. The philosophy which underlies the new education is unacceptable to a large number of Americans. The more intellectual critics are aware that this new education rests upon the philosophy of pragmatism, sometimes in the forms called instrumentalism or experimentalism. Although these philosophies are not well understood, many citizens have enough understanding to find them disquieting.

It is difficult to understand how any thoughtful educator can deny either of these contentions. Certainly the final control of all policy, including educational policy, under a representative government lies with the people. A clear distinction needs to be made between basic policy, on the one hand, and the techniques, or methodology, by which that policy is carried out. Such a distinction is sometimes difficult, but usually not impossible. The public will be wise to delegate problems of methodology to the professional group best able to decide them; determination of fundamental policy, however, cannot be so delegated.

This is true not merely of education but of all professions. In medicine the public is well-advised to leave methodological decisions to members of the medical profession. It is the physician who can best decide when an inflamed appendix should be removed and what instruments should be used in its removal; but in deciding whether an incurably ill individual should be put out of his misery, the physician must defer to the decision of the people through their legislatures, for this is a matter of broad public policy.

For example, the public may reasonably decide, as a matter of basic policy, that a child during the course of his education should gain a thorough knowledge of American institutions. The determination of the most effective method of teaching this history then becomes a professional problem best decided by professional teachers. If, however, the people come to the conclusion that children are completing school with an inadequate understanding of our institutions and the history of our nation, there is a danger that they will attempt through legislation (as they already have in some states) not only to require that a policy of teaching history be established but also to specify exactly *how* it shall be taught.

The charge that pragmatism has come to dominate educational thought in American education cannot easily be denied. Most educators will gladly admit the charge, contending that this is as it should be. The admission seems to suggest that pragmatism has become the new dogmatism, which is certainly not what James and Dewey, the leading pragmatic philosophers, intended. It is difficult to see how one can be dogmatic and pragmatic at the same time. But the courses in educational philosophy as taught in many teachers colleges lead students to the conviction that other patterns of thought are obsolete, that pragmatism is the new way of thinking. Informed people outside the field of education are pointing out that this may be the new way of thinking about the philosophical problems in educational circles, but that pragmatism has by no means supplanted other philosophies among contemporary philosophers or among thoughtful people in general.

Subsidiary to the two major criticisms, several minor but still important ones are widely heard. These may be summarized as follows:

1. Public education has extended itself to include many aspects of the child's life not formerly considered the province of the school, and this extension has taken place without full public approval.
2. The total effect of the new education is to leave the child, particularly the child of average or less than average intelligence, without a set of values.
3. Education has become anti-intellectual. It has tended to overemphasize large-muscle activity and to underemphasize cerebral activity. (It is probably a small minority that is unhappy about this trend, but it is an intelligent and vocal minority.)
4. Education as represented by textbooks, particularly in the social studies, has intentionally or unintentionally shown a generally consistent political list to the left. It is felt that the schools have properly taken a strong stand against fascism but have failed to take an equally strong stand against communism. (This criticism does not seem entirely consistent with items 2 and 3 above, but of course these criticisms are not all made by the same people and hence inconsistency is to be expected.)
5. It is widely believed that the children of this generation have failed to learn such skills as reading, oral and written expression, and computation as well as did their parents. (Perhaps this is one of the least supportable of all the criticisms, but it is the one most frequently heard and one to which we had better give some attention.)

It is my purpose in this book to examine these criticisms in the light of the changing conditions of the past fifty years. I shall not reject any of them without a very careful hearing.

I shall neither accept nor reject any educational principle or practice merely because it was first proposed by Dewey or by Kilpatrick, nor shall I accept or reject it because it is old or because it is new. The progressives have given much attention to the fact that antiquity is not a reliable basis for judging the soundness of an idea—neither is its newness.

Instead, I shall try to understand the current trends and the forces which have given rise to them. And I shall attempt to get back to first principles. For what is most needed in education today is a reexamination of first principles and then a reexamination of educational practices in the light of these principles. Such examination should involve the thinking of all teachers and of all others interested in the schools. It cannot be left to the professors of education in the universities and the teachers colleges, though, of course, they should participate.

Often the thoughtful citizen who is not an educator can see the big issues more clearly than can the teacher who is caught up in the complexities of his day-by-day classroom problems. But the citizen who is to take part in these discussions, however intelligent and well educated he may be, will need background knowledge of the schools which exist today. He will need some knowledge of the educational changes of recent years and of the philosophies which underlie these changes. He should have some information about the teachers colleges which prepare teachers for today's schools. It is hoped that this volume can help supply the background knowledge upon which the reexamination of the schools is to be based.

Such a reexamination as I am proposing must inevitably involve controversy, but I trust there will be no need for name calling. It is an unhappy fact that in some cities the controversy has already reached—in some cases has gone far beyond—that stage. Critics have loudly denounced the schools as godless, communistic, un-American, unenlightened, and subversive, while the defenders have counterattacked with charges that the critics themselves are fascist, reactionary, and, of course, un-American, unenlightened, and subversive.

In these unfortunate cities both the reasonable parents and the reasonable teachers are too busy dodging flying brickbats to have much opportunity to take a firm stand on anything themselves. The parent who makes a mild suggestion about the schools, that children should learn to spell, for example, may find himself identified with the most vicious of the schools' critics, and be so ruthlessly attacked that he is frightened into inarticulateness. The teacher who takes a clear stand on anything educational quickly learns to rush back to the relative security of the educational clichés.

It is my belief that the more violent participants in this controversy represent only a very small segment of the American public. It is my conviction that the great mass of thoughtful people, whether they be teachers, school administrators, school-board members, parents, or ordinary citizens, hold to neither extreme position. They criticize their schools and have every right to criticize them, just as they criticize and have a right to criticize their churches, their clubs, and their political parties. There is nothing either subversive or reactionary in their doing so.

But though we can admit that criticism is legitimate, it is clear that its nature has contributed to the confusion in the classroom. Today the teacher finds himself caught in a crossfire of conflicting demands.

Perhaps a part of the difficulty grows out of the American

people's exalted idea of the powers of formal education and lies in the exaggerated demands which they have made upon the schools—or upon the exaggerated claims which some educational leaders have made for education. A good deal of it, however, lies in the inconsistency of the demands. Critics have insisted, and quite rightly, upon the privilege of making the more basic decisions about educational policy; but they have failed to make those decisions. They have demanded more emphasis upon the fundamentals; but they have failed to decide among themselves what *is* fundamental.

The people have insisted upon the right of every youth to a high-school education; but they have inconsistently blamed the teachers for the lowering of academic standards which inevitably resulted. They have asked the schools to eliminate fads and frills. At the same time they have formed themselves into very powerful pressure groups which insist that the local high school maintain a winning football team and a marching band. They have insisted that we give greater attention to the problem of inculcating values; but when the teachers ask, "*Which* values?" the response is a babble of many voices. Finally, some of the critics have held the school responsible for the child's bad manners, for juvenile delinquency, for the high divorce rate, and for the popularity of horse-opera television.

If teachers are to provide the kind of schools which the people want for their children, the people must come to a decision and to some sort of tentative agreement. These decisions and these agreements must be communicated to the schools in such a way that it will be clear that they are decisions of the majority, arrived at democratically, and not the decisions of noisy minorities or pressure groups.

In the fall of 1950 *Life* asked Elmo Roper to conduct a nationwide survey to find out just where the people stood on controversial issues concerning the schools. The results of Roper's survey were published in its issue of October 16, 1950.

When Roper asked, "In general, would you say school children today are being taught more worthwhile and useful things than children were twenty years ago, not as worthwhile things, or about as worthwhile things as then?" 67 per cent of those questioned answered, "More worthwhile"; only 13 per cent said, "Not as worthwhile." The others didn't know or thought there had not been much change. This does not appear to represent any great dissatisfaction with the things being taught today. But when people were asked, "Taking everything into consideration, would you say that you are very satisfied, only fairly well satisfied, or not very satisfied with the public school system in your community?" only 33.4 per cent said, "Very satisfied"; 38.2 per cent said, "Only fairly satisfied"; 16.8 per cent said, "Not satisfied"; the other 11.6 per cent were uncertain. Perhaps the most significant aspect of the replies to this question was found in the breakdown on the basis of the educational level of the persons replying. Of persons with an eighth-grade education or less, only 13.4 per cent said they were "not satisfied," while of those with a college education, 24.2 per cent expressed themselves as "not satisfied" with the schools.

The greater dissatisfaction on the part of those with more educational background throws much light on the nature of the present criticism. For while some of it has seemed "crackpot" in nature, a great deal is of a very different kind. Much of it obviously is the criticism of intelligent and informed people, people whose judgments are not to be lightly waved aside.

As civilization moves forward and as populations increase, the problems confronting the schools increase in magnitude.

Though the schools should work for stability in an unstable world, they cannot themselves remain static, much less go backward.

I have no wish to return to the education of 1900 or to the education of the Middle Ages. While I am convinced that a better integration of knowledge is needed, I do not believe that an integration based upon scholasticism is likely to be acceptable to the majority of the American people. I have no wish to see the schools neglect the social and emotional development of children, and I do not think that the three R's are the only fundamentals.

I do not think that reading and discussing selections from one hundred or one thousand great books, or reading the entire book, is the total answer to our educational problems; although I wish that young people who are capable of grasping the ideas in these books could become more familiar with them, and I consider familiarity with such ideas essential to the teacher.

While I am convinced that every teacher should be a liberally educated person, I have seen little evidence that the liberal arts college, as now constituted, can provide better teachers than the colleges of education. But I do believe that the teachers college must revitalize itself, that it must become far more critical of its method and its philosophy than it recently has been.

Even those of us who believe that our schools have improved through the years can agree that there is still great room for further improvement. And perhaps we can agree that not all the changes of recent decades have been for the better. Surely we can agree that the contemporary scene in educational thinking is one of great confusion with no clear vision of the education which lies beyond the present controversy.

This book is intended as a first step in the search for the road ahead. It is written for all those citizens who must make the final decisions as to educational policy. Before the new road can be found it will be necessary to clear away a great deal of underbrush. If the brush cutting proves so great a task that the book never quite discloses the new road, the effort may nevertheless make it easier for others to find the way.

Some may wish to regard the point of view herein expressed as a "middle road," but it probably is more accurate to say that the effort is to find the new road wherever it may lie, provided only that it will lead us to the kind of America we all want for the coming years.

# CHAPTER II

# YESTERDAY AND TODAY

The most far-reaching changes which have occurred on the educational scene in recent decades are ones which cannot be attributed to Dewey or to the progressive movement. The most important of all changes has been the extension of universal education upward through the high school.

There has been no comparable recent change in the enrollment of the elementary school, for even before the turn of the century elementary education had become all but universal. Not all pupils completed the eighth grade, but by 1900 the child who did not attend school for at least six or seven years had become a rarity in all but a few remote sections of the country. Universal elementary education was an achievement of the nineteenth century.

The public high school began its development on a nationwide scale during the years immediately following the Civil War. But as late as 1900 not more than about 10 per cent of all boys and girls of high-school age attended such schools, and of these only about 70,000 graduated each year. By 1940 the number graduating annually had risen to over one million, or fifteen times as many as in 1900, although the total population had less than doubled. In 1940 about 75 per cent of all youths of high-school age were enrolled in school. Since World War II the proportion has continued to rise until high-school education has become an experience of almost every adolescent in many parts of the United States. It is this rise in high-school attendance which has brought us face to face with many of the problems which confront teachers today, and it is the failure adequately to solve these problems which has given rise to much of the criticism of the schools.

The three R's might conceivably provide a curricular basis for the elementary school, but it is much less clear that they can be the basis for secondary education. When only a few adolescents attended the secondary school, that school might legitimately base its curriculum upon college-entrance requirements, but such requirements are much less satisfactory as a curricular basis for a universal high school. Vocational education was not much of a problem in the elementary school or in the college preparatory school, but it is one which the universal high school cannot easily ignore.

Such controversial issues as those involved in sex education, the study of political ideologies, and the relationship between theories of evolution and religious beliefs would be much less serious if the public school had remained an elementary school for children under fourteen.

The extension of free and compulsory education to the secondary level may have been welcomed by professional educators, but it was not they who brought it about. It has come about as a result of social and economic forces beyond the control of any one professional group. These forces included the movement of populations from farm to city, the increased wealth of the nation, and the mechanization of industry with resultant technological unemployment.

When the population was predominantly rural, adolescents were needed at home to help their parents in the multitudinous duties of maintaining a farm and a farm home. But when many farm families moved to the city, the adolescent often became an unemployed roamer of the streets. As factories became more and more mechanized, he was less and less needed in the labor force even if he wished to find a job. Gradually he came to be excluded from the labor market by laws passed at the insistence of both labor groups and humanitarians who had observed some of the evil effects of factory labor upon juveniles. As homes accumulated more laborsaving appliances, the adolescent daughter was less needed by her mother as an assistant housekeeper.

Since 1920 farms too have become increasingly mechanized, so that the farmer has become less insistent upon keeping his son at home and more willing to have him attend high school. During these recent decades the wealth of the nation has increased enormously, so that it has become easier for us to support an extended school program. When we add to these factors the belief of the average American in both the economic and the social advantages of education beyond the elementary level, we see that the development of the universal high school was all but inevitable.

## II

The extension of universal education upward has led to a stress upon keeping all children in school. This has resulted indirectly in a change in our attitudes and practices regarding promotion from one grade to another. These practices always have differed from state to state and from city to city.

It is immediately apparent that the public schools of America are in no way uniform nor have they ever been. We have no national system of education as have many other countries. The Constitution of the United States does not mention education, and education has been left entirely to the various states or to the local communities. This has naturally led to a great variety of standards, of practices, and of philosophies. Such variety is not limited to education and is perhaps one of the essences of America. But our present problem is to seek the common factors, not the differences, and to observe these factors as they have changed over the years.

In my own first-grade class was one boy who was twelve years old. I shall call him Mortimer, hastening to add that the family relationship is not to the Adlers but to the Snerds. Mortimer sat awkwardly and uncomfortably in a seat much too small for him, his knees up under his chin, staring vacantly out of the window. At first he was admired by the smaller boys because he was stronger and was more skilled in the games played at recess. But before long we became aware of his limitations and he became the butt of our jokes. These he bore good-naturedly, for he had had six long years of experience with first-graders and accepted their humor with resignation. Mortimer was in the first grade for the simple reason that he could not learn to read, and until he learned to read he could not be promoted to the second grade.

When we visit the first grade of a school of 1953 we look in vain for the twelve-year-old Mortimer, and in our innocence we may at first think that the modern school has found ways of teaching him to read. But when we visit the sixth grade there he is, still staring vacantly out of the window and still unable to read. He is not socially accepted by the twelve-year-olds in his class and is the butt of their jokes. He undoubtedly still experiences such feelings of inferiority as are possible to him. But at least he is now in a seat which fits him.

The school has not solved the problem of dealing with the Mortimers. Some of the larger schools have provided a special class for him, but many modern educators abhor special classes because they set Mortimer apart and call attention to his limitations. Unfortunately, Mortimer was set apart by his inherited limitations and we have found no way of hiding these limitations from his schoolmates whether he is in a special class, the sixth grade, or the first grade.

The case of Mortimer points up one very real difference between the school of 1913 and the school of 1953. In 1913 promotion was made on the basis of the child's success in learning, without much attention to any other factor. In 1953 promotion is made on the basis of age, without much attention to any other factor. Whether or not this is progress is still being debated.

Some teachers will insist that their promotions are based upon a consideration of every aspect of the child's development, but such consideration is no solution to the problem. For while Mortimer is chronologically twelve years old, physically he is only eleven, socially he is nine, and intellectually he is perhaps seven or eight. If we add up all these figures and divide by four, we will place him in the third or fourth grade, a grade in which he fits in no respect. What most schools actually do is promote him one grade each year.

By this system of promotion he will, if he is patient or if the law requires him to remain in school, eventually graduate from high school. If his future employer assumes that graduation from high school means anything more than length of time served, he will be sadly disillusioned.

And in those states in which the only requirement for admission to the state university is high-school graduation, Mortimer may even enter college. Not that his experience with education will have endeared the schools to him, but if jobs are scarce or if no employer will have him he may find this the course of least resistance.

In each school there are but a few Mortimers, but for each

of these there are many children whose intellectual limitations make it impossible for them to do the academic work commonly expected of the average of their age groups. If promotions were based on accomplishments, some would be a year and some two years behind. The school which promotes on the basis of age alone is faced with a very difficult problem in dealing with these children. If all ten-year-olds are expected to perform in a manner reasonably expected of the average ten-year-old, the slow learners will encounter repeated experience with failure, and merely passing them at the end of the year will not conceal from them the fact that they have failed.

If the school does away with all ideas of expectations and requirements and adjusts the school program to the individual child, the result will be that a class will consist of thirty or forty individuals, each occupied with a different task. Some teachers profess to do this, and with a class of twelve or fifteen children such individualization of instruction might conceivably be possible. But with today's average class of thirty-five children it simply cannot be done. What usually happens is that the teacher assigns a task (no progressive teacher would ever be caught *assigning* a task but, as we will see, most schools are not consistently progressive), accepts a mediocre performance from the average and the superior pupils, and accepts a less than mediocre response from the less able. Then at the end of the year all are moved to the next grade just as though their attainments had been equal.

In an earlier day slow-learning children would have been held back a year or two and then would have dropped out of school to go to work at the age of fourteen or fifteen. But the extension of universal education to the secondary level, the raising of the upper age limit for compulsory education, and the legal prohibitions placed upon child labor have made the continuation of this course unfeasible. It is most unlikely that either the humanitarians or the labor unions will ever permit the lowering of the age limit for gainful employment.

The superior child in a classroom of average children is less conspicuous than is the slow learner, but the problems he presents are even more important. The schools have never done a very good job of dealing with him. A generation or two ago he was permitted to skip a grade, but when this was done more than once or twice he found himself with a group so much more mature than he physically and socially that this solution sometimes did more harm than good. A boy of fourteen in a class in which the girls are seventeen or eighteen does not find it easy to become a normal male adult. But the contemporary custom of keeping the bright boy with his age group leads to his moving through school without ever meeting a real intellectual challenge. He learns to get by with a minimum of effort. If he does better thinking than is required of him he may get a little praise from his teacher; but he would much rather be praised by youths of his own age, and he finds that their praise is much more easily achieved by becoming a cheer leader, a quarterback, or an expert on bebop. So the bright boy or girl in the typical high school learns to be energetic in all activities except the intellectual. All too often both teachers and parents advise him not to read so much and to get out and mix more with people.

Although this system of universal promotions is one of the most common bases for criticism of the schools, no one seems to have a very sound solution for the problem. But educators have made a very serious mistake in pretending that promoting everyone on an age basis has solved it. We will be on much safer ground if we simply admit that some of the results are bad but that we don't know what to do about it.

Surely we must call a halt somewhere. The governor of one of our states has announced that every young man and woman in his state has a *right* to a college education. His is a state in which all high-school graduates are now admitted to the state colleges and the state university; it therefore appears that these colleges will be falling down on their job if they do not permit all students to continue to the bachelor's degree. Following this line of reasoning, are we someday to promote pupils through engineering school, medical, and law schools on the basis of years of attendance?

At some point we must do an about-face. We must say clearly that beyond this point the student may be promoted only on the basis of demonstrated competence, that beyond this point his own interests must be subordinated to those of the community which he is to serve as an adult.

### III

But there remains the problem of what to do about promotions in the elementary school and the high school. Some basic decisions must be reached—decisions consistent with the facts and acceptable to the majority.

The problem of promotions is closely related to that of grades. Older readers will recall the day when school grades were based upon a scale of 0 to 100, and these figures were usually listed as percentages. What they were percentages of was never very clear. In the case of spelling, the grade sometimes meant percentages of assigned words which the pupil had spelled correctly, but in such subjects as history and literature it could have had no such meaning. I recall that once as a fourth-grader I received a grade of 60 per cent in "deportment." It is clear that this grade indicated some dissatisfaction on the part of the teacher, and that I still recall it may be related to the fact that my parents too expressed dissatisfaction—not with the teacher but with me. But I wonder what the grade of 60 was a percentage of. Did it mean that I had behaved myself, according to her standards, 60 per cent of the time? I doubt it. In fact I very much doubt that she had any idea at all what it meant, except that my conduct had been unsatisfactory.

When we had percentage grades some arbitrary figure was usually selected as the passing grade and in many schools this figure was pegged at 70 per cent. But this really didn't make much sense. A student who understood 70 per cent of the ideas in a difficult history book might be a very good student indeed, but you would hardly wish to hire as a secretary a girl who spelled correctly only 70 per cent of the words used in a letter. Nor would you wish to employ as a bookkeeper a boy who could find the correct total to a column of figures 70 per cent of the time.

These complications have led, in most places, to an abandonment of the percentage system of grading. The system which most frequently replaced it was one in which letters—A, B, C, D, and F—were used.

F meant that the work done had fallen below the minimum standards set by the teacher or the school and that a repetition of the work or of the school grade would be necessary. D meant that the pupil had skimmed by, but by a close margin. In many high schools and colleges it meant that it would be necessary for him to do better work in other courses to compensate for the D since colleges particularly often require a C average for graduation.

A grade of C supposedly meant average work, although many an amiable teacher found himself giving more B's than C's. But a B was supposed to mean better than average work, while an A meant that the work had been excellent.

This grading system is still used in a great many colleges and in some high schools, but it is becoming increasingly rare in elementary schools. It had some real defects, but the systems which have replaced it have not always been satisfactory to either parents or teachers.

In place of the grading systems, many schools, particularly elementary schools, have substituted new practices in great variety. Some of them report to parents through individual conferences between teacher and parents. Others still use report cards, but number or letter grades have been replaced by adjectives or adverbs—excellent, good, fair, average, and the like. In still other schools the teachers write short essays or character sketches: "Junior is showing improvement in his understanding of numbers but he still has some difficulty with his reading. He tries hard to be a good citizen but he forgets occasionally and pushes little girls into mud puddles." This last is the present-day equivalent of my 60 per cent in deportment. It has the advantage of giving the parent a better insight into the nature of Junior's conduct, although it provides little understanding of the cause of his misbehavior.

But verbal reports of the child's success in learning the three R's have not proved satisfactory to parents. The fact that Junior is "improving" in his understanding of numbers tells the parent no more than did the fact that a boy in my day received a grade of 75 in arithmetic in January and a grade of 82 in February. It tells even less about the success he is having in coming up to the standards of his grade or in competing with other children in his class.

The abandonment of competitive grades has been based in large part upon the belief of many contemporary educational leaders that competition among school children does more harm than good and that no uniform standards should be set for children of different abilities and backgrounds. We shall return to a discussion of these convictions and the basis for them, but first let us ask why grades or reports should be used at all.

There appear to be at least four possible answers to the question "Why should schools give grades?"

1.  The parents wish to have a report from the teacher on the child's progress.
2.  A grading system, properly administered, provides the child with additional motivation. Such motivation supplements the motivation provided by the child's interest in the work.
3.  Grades which become a part of the permanent records are one of the teacher's methods of informing the principal, other teachers, and, in the case of older children, potential employers, of the student's achievements.
4.  Grades are necessary in determining the child's readiness for advancement to the next level of education.

Those who have led the movement to do away with grades have offered the following arguments against their use.

1.  There is a good deal of evidence that grades are notoriously unreliable.
2.  Instead of providing motivation for effective learning, grades have often motivated the child to discover ways of getting high grades without learning. In some cases the effect has been to encourage dishonesty.
3.  Children who possess inferior intellectual ability or who have specific emotional blocks are sometimes punished by their parents for receiving low grades, and in some cases such punishment only serves to intensify the child's emotional conflict and his dislike for school without helping him to discover or to correct the sources of his inadequacy.
4.  At best, the meaning of a grade is so vague in the minds of children, parents, teachers, and everyone else that the grade is almost useless.

Let us discuss each of these in turn.

When an educator says that grades are unreliable he means that the same piece of schoolwork, if judged by several different teachers, will not be given the same grade by all the teachers, or that the same work, if submitted to the teacher by several different children, will receive various grades. There is a good deal of impressive evidence, experimental in nature, that this is true. This evidence has been widely published in educational journals and college textbooks and is familiar to many teachers though probably less well known outside the teaching profession. I once conducted a simplified form of such an experiment, using as subjects a class of experienced teachers who were enrolled in a summer-session course in education. Twenty teachers of the upper elementary school level were asked to grade the papers of some seventh-grade sudents. The papers were from an arithmetic class, and this subject was chosen deliberately because arithmetic is supposed to be a subject in which answers are either right or wrong without room for subjective judgment on the part of the teacher. But let us look at the results.

The questions were chosen from a standard textbook. The first question was stated as follows: "A farmer has found that a 10-acre pasture lot provides forage for 17 cows. How many cows can be pastured on a lot of 15 acres?"

The first pupil gave as his answer, "25½ cows." The twenty teachers were asked to indicate what grade—on a scale of 0 to 100—should be given for this answer.

Fourteen of the teachers gave the pupil a grade of 100 per cent. Three gave him a zero, one gave 50 per cent, one 70 per cent, and one 90 per cent. I discovered that one of the teachers had given a grade of zero because he had himself made an error in computing the correct answer. Of this teacher the less said the better. We all make mistakes; some of us made our first mistake when we decided to become teachers.

The other five teachers who gave less than a perfect score for the answer of 25½ cows justified their decision by pointing out that there is no such thing as half a cow, or if there is, the half cow is already past the stage of needing pasture. One of these teachers thought the correct answer should be 26, that being the next largest whole number. The others thought the correct answer should be 25. Those who gave grades of zero said that an answer to a problem in arithmetic was always either right or wrong. The one who gave a grade of 90 per cent thought it more reasonable to take off 10 per cent than to give a grade of zero for a solution in which the computation of fractions had been accurately done.

The second problem was stated this way: "If a man earns $1.15 per hour, what is his pay for a 40-hour week?" The student experienced difficulty in locating the decimal point and came up with the remarkable answer of $460.00.

Twelve of the teachers gave him a zero. But four gave him 50 per cent, three gave him 80 per cent, and one gave him a grade of 90 per cent. Those who gave grades higher than zero thought a student who had trouble with a slippery decimal point but who had otherwise multiplied correctly should receive a higher grade than would be given to students who came up with such totally erroneous answers as $17.60, $87.00, or with the correct but inadequate answer, "I don't know." Some thought the student should be given some credit for effort, and others stressed the importance of giving a grade which would encourage and motivate him.

It is obvious that the scholastic standing of this student will depend to a very large degree upon the chance factor of which teacher happens to preside over his classroom. This, in part, is what we mean by the unreliability of grades.

The objection that grades sometimes lead to dishonesty is easily documented. All of us can recall instances in which we or our schoolmates found ways of cheating. Even schools and colleges which make use of the honor system are not always free from such difficulty. A dean of a well-known college which follows such a system admits privately that the honor system does not work in his school. Many students complain that cheating is widespread but that honest students are unwilling to report the practice, as the rules require, lest they be accused of "squealing." This dean says that they would like to discard the honor system and go back to supervised examinations but dare not do so because such a change would be an admission that some students are dishonest; such an admission would gain widespread publicity and would do great damage to the name of the college.

The cheating scandals at West Point made it clear that even military schools, with their great emphasis on honor, have their difficulties. But at least the West Point officials, when dishonesty was discovered, dealt with the problem with a courage and dispatch which few college deans would dare emulate.

It is probably true that the elimination of grades would do much to eliminate cheating in examinations. But to some it seems that taking away all temptation is a poor way to develop character.

It is true that the child who by reason of intellectual inferiority, or for any other reason, persistently receives low grades often develops feelings of inferiority and of conflict and antagonism toward teachers and schools. There is no doubt either that such feelings seriously interfere with the child's normal personality development.

Some teachers have concluded that children should be graded upon the basis of their own improvement rather than upon a comparison with other children. This does indeed have some advantages. The child thus graded is like a golfer who concerns himself only with his own daily score and ignores the scores of other golfers. As long as his own score shows improvement he is motivated to continue his efforts. But this technique will work only so long as he can avoid playing in company with other golfers, because the moment he enters a foursome he finds it impossible to avoid comparison.

The criticism that grades are made almost useless by the vagueness of their meaning is not easily answered. It is quite true that some grades represent facts learned, others represent broader understandings gained, effort expended, enthusiasm evidenced, or conformity to the wishes of the teacher. Some grades represent the teacher's judgment of the child's probable ability to get along at the succeeding level of education. Some are predictions of future vocational success. Some are judgments regarding the child's creative ability.

In this matter of grades there is great need for clarification. Every grade card or record book should be headed with some such statement as "These grades represent percentage of correct answers on objective tests," or "These grades represent the child's position in relation to other members of his class in academic achievement," or "These grades indicate the amount of improvement which the child has shown as compared to his own previous record," or even "These grades are teachers' judgments of the child's personality and character traits."

The teaching profession itself may reasonably decide what records should be kept of each child's progress and the form which these records should take. The reports made to parents are quite another matter.

If the parent is dissatisfied with the current trend away from grades and toward the use of verbalized reports, he is well within his rights if he makes his dissatisfaction known. This is one of the matters that may be discussed in parent-teacher meetings or in other groups in which parents, teachers, and school administrators are present.

The discussion will almost certainly get back to the matter of the philosophy of the school, because the change in the grading system is a reflection of a change in educational philosophy. To understand this change we must give some attention to the influence of John Dewey.

# CHAPTER III

# THE SHADOW OF JOHN DEWEY

If an institution is but the lengthened shadow of a man, few men have cast a larger shadow than John Dewey; the shadow is the American public school. But in many areas where the outline of the man is clear, the shadow is hazy, its outlines fuzzy. Even if the shadow were a sharp one, there are many who would regard it with alarm, though few of these have recently found their way to professorships of education.

John Dewey is considered by many, even of those who disagree with him—Bertrand Russell, for example—to be America's greatest philosopher. Certainly he is its most influential. His influence in America and throughout the world extends far beyond the bounds of education.

Dewey first gained fame as an educational philosopher while a member of the faculty of the University of Chicago, a fact which must have caused considerable embarrassment, in later years, to Mr. Hutchins. But Dewey's lengthening shadow did not become fully apparent until he moved, in 1904, to Columbia University. His enormous influence was felt through Teachers College of that university, which, during his years at Columbia, became the mecca of the teachers of teachers.

In many a college of education one-fourth to one-half of the faculty members have, at some time, studied at Teachers College, Columbia, and many of the others have taken part or all their graduate work at universities whose professors of education had earlier sat at the feet of Dewey and his disciples.

It is often the fate of a great thinker that, as his fame grows, his followers more and more come to worship him without bothering to understand him. Thus it becomes possible for those who call themselves his followers to deviate markedly from his teachings while still kneeling at the altar which they have erected to his memory. This was true of the followers of Plato and of many great men since his time. But Dewey differs from his predecessors in an important respect. In the case of most philosophers the deification did not occur until long after the great man was dead; in the case of Dewey it occurred while he was still alive.

The reason is not hard to find. Dewey's essential originality lies in his epistemology, his interpretation of the nature of knowing and the meaning of truth; and this aspect of Dewey's teaching is incredibly difficult for most of us to comprehend. Its understanding calls for a very superior intellect, a considerable knowledge of philosophic terminology, and the willingness to give it a great deal of careful thought. It is not surprising that most of the teachers who follow methods whose justification lies in Dewey's epistemology have no comprehension whatever of the philosophical basis for these assumptions.

None of the simplified explanations of pragmatism have been acceptable to Dewey. When popularizers interpreted the term "pragmatic" as meaning "practical" and said, "If it works, it's good," William James did not object very seriously; he wanted his to be a philosophy of the market place and did not worry about the vulgarization of it. But Dewey would have none of such simplifications. To avoid them he abandoned the word "pragmatism" in his later works and substituted "instrumentalism," which he felt was less likely to lead to oversimplification. Dewey never stated his definition of instrumentalism in a way that would be easily understandable to the average man. He probably considered it impossible to make such a statement.

Not all of Dewey is so difficult to understand as is his epistemology. There are two John Deweys. One is the Dewey who wrote the clear and understandable *Experience and Education*. This Dewey sounds to us like a wise and fatherly old man of long experience and a great deal of common sense, talking about practical problems.

The other Dewey is Dewey the philosopher, the author of such erudite tomes as *Logic: The Theory of Inquiry* and *Essays in Experimental Logic*. This Dewey is profound and scholarly, but often recondite to the point of obscurity. Some of his disciples will deny the obscurity, but it is these same disciples who accuse Russell and Santayana (who, whether or not you approve of them, are surely among the great intellects of our times) of misunderstanding Dewey.

If some of the better contemporary minds experience difficulty in understanding Dewey's epistemology and are accused of misinterpreting his meaning, it is presumptuous indeed for this writer to try to explain his concepts to the reader. However, to ignore the problem of interpretation seems an unjustifiable evasion in view of our problem which is that of understanding contemporary education.

Epistemology is an attempt to answer the questions: What is truth? What can we know? How do we know? Numerous answers have been given. Some have held that knowledge may be mystical, *i.e.*, knowledge is communicated directly to us by unknown means from a divine or unknown source. Conscience is an example, revelation another. Others have agreed with Locke that all knowledge must come through the sense organs;

the mind at birth is a blank slate upon which experience writes. This is empiricism. Still others hold that knowledge is rational. By the process of reasoning we may arrive at newly discovered truths—truths which did not reach us through our senses. The scientific method accepts data from empirical sources and then uses the rational method, employing either verbal or mathematical symbols, to arrive at generalizations.

Each set of epistemological assumptions has implications for education. If knowledge is primarily rational, the schools should devote most of their time to the development of skill in reasoning. In such a school Socrates would be the ideal teacher.

If knowledge is exclusively empirical, education must consist of providing the child with maximum opportunity for sensory experience. He must be given every possible opportunity to see, to hear, to taste, to smell, and to feel.

If knowledge is both empirical and rational, the schools should make sure that the child has ample sensory experiences, either in or out of school, and that the child learns to deal with these experiences rationally so that he may arrive at generalizations, or higher truths.

In so far as knowledge has mystical origins there appears to be little need for a teacher, unless it is assumed that the teacher's mystical knowledge is better or more complete than that of the child. If you are to let your conscience be your guide and if your conscience has origins which are neither empirical nor rational, there is not much need for education. But probably no one contends that *all* knowledge is mystical.

Dewey holds that all of these assumptions about truth are incomplete and misleading. For Dewey, truth is "warranted assertability." He agrees with Peirce that truth is whatever in the long run is agreed upon by those who investigate. Mount Everest has no "true" height which is independent of the measurements made of it. So long as all investigators agreed that its elevation above sea level is 29,002 feet, that was its true elevation. If, after making new measurements, they agree that its height is 30,000 feet, that becomes the true height. To a realist it seems that Everest has a true height which remains constant, except for the possibility of an actual elevation of the land mass, regardless of any errors in trigonometry; but this is not so to Dewey. Truth, he says, is progressive and flexible. Ideas are *instruments* whereby the individual maintains a satisfactory relationship with his environment. If I live in a world in which 29,002 feet is accepted as Everest's height, my acceptance of this as a fact enables me to establish such a relationship.

Dewey holds that all scientific propositions are merely predictions and all logical propositions must be tested in terms of their consequences. If certain operations are performed, certain phenomena will be observed. Pragmatists are very fond of the subjunctive.

"Inquiry," says Dewey, "is the controlled or directed transformation of an indeterminate situation into one that is so determinate in its constituent distinctions and relations as to convert the elements of the original situation into a unified whole."

And again, "The essence of pragmatic instrumentalism is to conceive of *both* knowledge and practice as a means of making goods—excellences of all kinds—secure in experienced existence" (John Dewey, *The Quest for Certainty*, Minton, Balch & Co., New York, 1929, p. 47).

Perhaps you are one of the fortunate few to whom the above is perfectly clear. But if not, you have considerable company; and many members of this company are teachers in very progressive schools.

Dewey's concept of values—and this concept is of course the basis for his ethics—is not quite so difficult as is his epistemology. Even so, it is not easy to reduce this concept to terms which are readily understandable to those of us who are not philosophers, nor is it likely that we can give a simple explanation which will be entirely aceptable to Dewey's followers.

Pragmatic values are rooted in the activities whereby an individual establishes a satisfactory relationship with his social environment. Values do not consist of adherence to any fixed set of rules or standards but involve a constant adjustment to individual and social needs.

Some educators seem to believe that pragmatism and relativism are synonymous as applied to ethical values, but it is entirely possible to hold that values are relative without assuming that they must be derived pragmatically. Some relativists hold with Bentham and Mill that ethics should be based upon the greatest good of the greatest number; others believe that ethics consists solely of conformity to the mores of whatever group one happens to be a part.

I think Dewey would have denied that mere conformity is necessarily a satisfactory relationship. But pragmatic ethics involves the process of resolving the conflict between the individual's urges or needs and the dictates of the social group with a view to action which will contribute to the individual's adjustment to the group. Thus, to go back to the epistemology, an indeterminate situation is transformed into a determinate one. In other words, something is accomplished, a decision is reached, action follows.

Pragmatic ethics must be separately derived by the individual for himself. Or perhaps the derivation can involve a group process with individual variations. This operational development of a value system may be possible for a philosopher, but it is a good deal to ask of a small child, particularly if the teacher does not have a very clear idea of the processes involved.

It is really not surprising that in many schools the old system of values, based upon rules and standards passed down from the elders, has been thrown out and nothing put in its place.

Some of us who occasionally share the pragmatists' doubts about the wisdom of the elders, and who have no fondness for rigid rules, still are skeptical about the child's ability to develop his own value system without a good deal of assistance.

But the widespread acceptance by teachers of Dewey as their leader may not to any great extent have been based upon either his epistemology or his value system.

It is significant that Dewey's ideas have been most widely accepted as a basis for education in the elementary school, have gained slower acceptance in the high school, and until recently have had comparatively little influence upon the colleges. This is no accident. For it seems safe to assume that the individual's choice of a personal philosophy, or of a philosophy upon which to base his professional decisions, often is made more on the basis of his psychology rather than on the basis of cold logic. We choose such beliefs as reinforce our egos. This is particularly true of those who suffer from feelings of inferiority. And in the past the elementary teacher often has been made to feel inferior to those who teach older children and adolescents.

So long as it was held that education consisted in large part of passing along organized knowledge, it seemed to follow that teachers who dealt with older and more mature minds had greater responsibilities and should therefore be selected more carefully, should be paid more, and should enjoy higher prestige than those who dealt with infants. A hierarchy developed in education in which the graduate-school professor stood at the top of the pyramid and the nursery-school teacher at the bottom. This was reflected in the salary scales. No one questioned that a Harvard professor was more important to society and should receive a much higher salary than a teacher in the elementary school.

But Dewey's interpretations of the nature of education, if carried to their logical conclusions, would change all that. The essence of education is not the unit of knowledge but the activity of the learner. The child's activities and experiences are no less important than are those of the graduate student, and the teacher who guides those activities is no less important than is the university professor. No one assumes that the pediatrician is less important or should be paid less or enjoy less prestige than the gerontologist merely because he works with less mature human beings.

Some progressive educators went even farther. They proposed that the elementary school, which received the child during his most impressionable years, was even more important than the high school or the college. Many elementary teachers came to speak scornfully of the academicians and the professors and to regard them as a great barrier in the path of educational progress. In many public schools, particularly in the West, the conviction that the elementary teacher is at least as important as is the teacher of adolescents has been implemented by salary schedules which give the same pay to teachers at all levels, from the kindergarten through the junior college. Is it any wonder that the primary-school teacher, hitherto scorned, neglected, and underpaid, came to love Dewey while the professors continued to ignore him?

But while it is easy to understand the basis for Dewey's acceptance, it does not necessarily follow that this basis establishes the superiority of his philosophy of education. Though his philosophy is sometimes difficult to comprehend, one thing is clear: If we are to test Dewey's hypothesis, by that same hypothesis we shall judge it in terms of the effect which it has had. In dealing with our present problem this means testing it in terms of the way it has influenced actual practices in the schools. No good pragmatist can very well object to that. Let us look at the schools which have been influenced by Dewey.

Dewey's influence on the public schools was indirect and involved the passing of his ideas through the minds of a hierarchy of educators. Such transmission of ideas is an interesting process, particularly when the various minds involved are not of equal perspicacity.

Dewey said, "We learn by doing." This was interpreted by Kilpatrick and other, lesser, disciples at Columbia's Teachers College to their students who then secured positions in the teachers colleges throughout the country. These professors then passed the word, along with their own interpretations, to prospective teachers who, according to their lights, attempted to apply the concept in their own classrooms. In too many cases the only result was that the children moved around more and read less.

This was not at all what Dewey had in mind. Dewey, who in his day made significant contributions to the psychology of learning, was well aware that thinking and reading are forms of doing. To Dewey a child reading a book is "doing." But he learns not what is in the book but what he "does" in response to the printed page. A youth taking part in a Socratic dialogue is "doing." He learns what he does; that is, he learns to think and to talk.

What Dewey did wish to emphasize was that the child who is required to read something beyond his comprehension or who is expected to listen to a lecture that is far over his head learns not what is in the book or what is being said in the lecture but whatever he actually is doing. In this case he probably learns to daydream. Dewey was convinced that the elementary school was setting unrealistic standards for the intellectual or symbolic activities of many children and he was quite willing to see children move about more in the classroom. But he never questioned that intellectual activity is educative, particularly for more mature minds. It was Dewey himself who said, "Theory is, in the end, the most practical of all things." And Dewey continued to use the lecture method in his own teaching without apologizing for it.

But the disciples became hopelessly confused by this "learn by doing" concept and were forced by circumstance to be most inconsistent. The writer has many times been amused to hear speakers at educational conferences lecture endlessly about the evils of the lecture system and receive very good pay for it too.

There is little doubt that symbolic or verbal activity has often been overemphasized, particularly in the elementary school, and that such activity frequently has failed to stimulate the responses expected of the pupil. But it does not at all follow that such activities should be avoided altogether, even in the primary grades. Nor does it follow that overt physical activity is more important than cerebral activity. Those things which involve muscular activity—sawing a board, or repairing a tire—are best learned through such activity. But if the child is to gain an understanding of the history of Western civilization, the "doing" involved must include a great deal of reading, talking, listening, looking at pictures, and just plain thinking. Perhaps he can learn a little by building a mud replica of a medieval castle on a sand table, but it is very doubtful if the time is as profitably spent as it would be in reading a good history book, even though the reading does not involve activity of the large muscles. The child can perhaps learn a little something of biology by going down to the seashore to peer under a wet rock, but such activities had better be supplemented by a good deal of reading if he is to get the big ideas. Of course we are assuming that he *can* read and read well. If he cannot, the school had better get to work on that.

Dewey said, "Education is growth." By the time this had gone through channels the meaning had become so confused that many teachers took it to mean that learning was no longer important, that Dewey had discovered something called "growth" which was neither maturation nor learning but which superseded both. Indeed, even professors of education and many of the writers of the textbooks seemed to share this confusion. Books on the psychology of learning, educational psychology, and child psychology were replaced by books entitled *Child Growth* or *Child Growth and Development*, and some of these curious volumes gave little or no attention to the theory and techniques of learning.

To psychologists who gave any attention to this development—and psychologists who were working in teachers colleges could not ignore it—the result seemed to be utter confusion. Growth had always had a clear meaning. It referred to changes which took place as a result of maturational processes. To the psychologist it meant exactly what it still means to the biologist.

Learning stands in contrast to growth or maturation. Learning is dependent upon maturation but is, nevertheless, a separate process. Learning refers to those relatively stable changes in response patterns which result from the individual's experiences. We learn to talk, we learn the multiplication table, we learn table manners—and some of us learn to be neurotic. None of these responses can occur through maturation or growth alone. To the psychologist it seemed that all this emphasis on growth and the neglect of an understanding of the learning process left the prospective teacher completely unprepared for his job. Two distinct concepts had been replaced by one fuzzy one. At least one progressive educator, Bode, became aware of this confusion, for he said in 1938, "The doctrine of growth, in its present form, becomes a positive obstacle to clear thinking on the part of the teacher" (Boyd H. Bode, *Progressive Education at the Crossroads*, Newson & Company, New York, 1938, p. 78). But most educators have continued to use the term.

When he described education as growth, Dewey meant that education is the process of arriving at maturity. He knew that arriving at maturity, in the social sense, involved both maturation and learning, but there was no available word that adequately covered the two and he thought "growth" would convey the idea. He had some justification in the use of this word, as it had long been used in literature with this generalized meaning. He wanted to emphasize the dependence of learning on maturation. A child cannot learn to read or to solve algebraic equations until certain maturations have taken place. But he surely did not mean that an understanding of the learning process should be neglected in the teachers colleges. If he became aware of the effect of his words on the curriculums in teacher education, he must have been appalled; but it appears that in his later years Dewey was almost out of touch with what was going on in most teachers colleges. These colleges worshiped him at a distance, often without reading what he had said. He became a remote god, understood, if at all, only through the interpretations of his disciples. And unfortunately, some of his disciples were conspicuous more for their devotion and enthusiasm than for their clear thinking.

Dewey said, "Education is a social process." By the time this had reached the classroom it had taken on two somewhat illogical interpretations. It was taken to mean, first, that *all* educational activities must be social in nature and, second, that since the extrovert personality functions more easily in social situations than does the introvert, an effort should be made to help all children to become extroverted. The child who preferred the contemplative life must at all costs be brought out of his seclusion and thrust into strenuous social activity. If he wished to read poetry when other children were playing drop the handkerchief, the teacher first made an effort to entice or to force him into the more social activity, and if this failed she sent out a call for the school psychologist.

In doing this she was not always mistaken, for it is true that the seriously withdrawn child often needs professional help. The withdrawn child or adolescent is, in the long run, more likely to become a serious psychological problem than is the mildly aggressive child, because excessive withdrawing is not ordinarily self-corrective. Sometimes withdrawing is the first symptom of serious psychological conflicts of the kind which may lead to neurosis, and occasionally it presages a developing psychosis of the schizoid variety. But such serious tendencies to withdraw are not materially helped when a teacher takes the child by the hand and leads him or forces him into the very social situation which he is trying to avoid.

And it is a very serious error to assume that the child who now and then likes to take solitary walks, to be alone with a good book when others are playing boisterous games, or to play alone with mechanical gadgets or scientific instruments is necessarily withdrawn in any abnormal or undesirable sense. In many cases it would be more accurate to say simply that this child is self-sufficient, and in many cases it would be wiser to encourage him in his self-sufficiency, for even our complex society needs self-sufficient people who can happily and effectively work in solitude. It is unlikely that the work of many of our finest poets, composers, inventors, and experimental scientists could have been accomplished by extroverts. If Emily Dickinson and Thomas Edison had been brought out of their seclusion, had been cured of their preference for solitude, we might have been deprived of some beautiful poetry and perhaps denied the electric light. And there is certainly room for debate as to whether they would in the long run have been happier persons. The extrovert makes a better salesman than does the introvert, but not all of our children are destined to become salesmen.

It is important that the teacher recognize the child who has great need of social participation but who is afraid to take his place in the group because of lack of some necessary skill or because of past experience with being rejected by the group. The teacher can help such a child to become an accepted member of the group. But it is time for us to reject the notion that every normal boy must love to play football, that every normal adolescent must revel in square dancing, and that every normal adult must enjoy going to conventions.

The statement that education is a social process is a dangerous and misleading half truth. Some education is social; some education must be solitary and individual.

Dewey said, "Education is not preparation for life, education is life itself." When this had gone through the long and circuitous route to the classroom it was understood to mean that the school should not be overly concerned with preparing the child for anything except possibly the strenuous social activity which we have mentioned. The high school should not worry about whether it was preparing the student for college, and the elementary school should not concern itself with preparing the child for high school. Neither should give much thought to preparing him for adult responsibilities. The school was to be merely a specialized environment in which the child lived and grew. One would think that the teachers had been brought up on an intellectual diet consisting exclusively of Rousseau's *Émile*.

Dewey's intention was to break the strangle hold which he was convinced the colleges had upon the curriculum of the high school and which adult requirements had placed upon all levels of education. He wanted the curriculum to be based upon the present needs of children and to be adjusted to their actual capacities rather than to assumed capacities.

He probably wished also to emphasize his view that the happiness of the child should not be sacrificed to a type of schooling which he found distasteful, but which was justified on the basis of the preparation which it presumably gave him for later years. On this many of us can agree. Sound education need not be an unpleasant experience for the learner. Many aspects of education will be more, rather than less, effective if they are enjoyed by the learner. But in education, as in every other aspect of life, it is sometimes necessary to sacrifice immediate pleasures for more lasting satisfactions.

To be sure, the school years are a portion, an important portion, of life. But it is equally true that education must be a preparation for later life. If the child emerges from the public school no better prepared for adult life than he would have been had he never gone to school, the taxpayers are being taken for a very expensive ride.

Dewey said, "Education must concern itself with the whole child." His meaning was that the education of the past had, in his opinion, been too exclusively intellectual. Consistent with his functional interpretation of psychology, he wished to emphasize the view that intellectual development cannot take place apart from emotional, social, and physical development. His followers interpreted this to mean that the school should give more attention than it had in the past to these other aspects of the child's development. But by the time this idea had filtered down to the classroom level it was widely taken to mean that all aspects of development are of *equal* importance, something that Dewey surely never intended.

This belief that all educational activities are of equal or nearly equal value has now extended itself to the colleges and is clearly reflected in their catalogues. I select one of these catalogues at random and find it is that of a typical Middle Western school. This college offers only one course in the psychology of learning; for this the student, if he passes the examination, receives three credits toward graduation. There are five courses in square dancing for which he receives five credits without being troubled by an examination. A study of Shakespeare's tragedies yields three credits; basket weaving, two credits; basic news writing, five credits; basic shorthand, three credits; campcraft, three credits; pottery making, three credits; American government, three credits; small-boat building, five credits; and ethics, three credits. I have no desire to deride any of these academic offerings; no doubt each can be defended. But it seems most unlikely that anyone whose thinking has not been softened up by current educational trends can consider them of equal or nearly equal value in their contribution to the development of the "whole man." And if they are not of equal value they should not receive equal credit toward a college degree, if that degree is to have any educational significance. It seems most improbable that the teacher who graduates from this college is prepared to make wise judgments as to the relative value of the various aspects of the educational experiences of children.

I once visited a workshop in which a group of teachers were discussing the problem of what is important in education. Some of the teachers had come through universities, some through private liberal arts colleges, and others through teachers colleges, but all had had the conventional indoctrination in contemporary educational philosophy. One teacher started the discussion by saying, "It seems to me that the healthful emotional development of the child is just as important as is his learning of subject matter." Everyone present agreed with this fully. Another said, "But man is a social animal, and it is equally important for him to learn to get along with people." Again the agreement was unanimous. A third said, "I teach physical education and know from my own experience that unless the child is healthy and well developed physically he cannot be considered well educated." Again they agreed. A fourth said, "Let us not forget music. After all the appreciation of fine music and ability to sing or to play an instrument are just as important as any of the things we have mentioned." More agreement. A fifth teacher asked, "But what good are all these things if one cannot make a living? Surely vocational training is equally important." They all nodded emphatically. They agreed too on the equal importance of recreation, of art, and of leisure-time activities. The final conclusion seemed to be that all things are equally important and that some things might be "even more equally important" than others.

The trend taken by this discussion represents not so much a complete denial of values, as a reluctance to disagree with anyone in the group. The unwillingness to disagree seems to have become one of the trade-marks of contemporary education. In workshops, seminars, and educational conferences cooperation is stressed above all things. The aim of each such gathering is an agreement and a reaffirmation.

The individual who persistently holds to a minority point of view is treated as a backward child who must be brought to see the light. The others may be patient with him and may be willing to give a great deal of time to discussion, but they make it clear that in the end he must come to agreement with the group. Permanent nonagreement is never tolerated. It is no exaggeration to say that if a Socrates, a Hobbes, or a Locke sat with such a group, the educators would give no real consideration to his suggestions. They would devote all their energies to convincing him that his concepts were old-fashioned (and hence erroneous) and to converting him to the new philosophy.

An examination of the professional journals, particularly those published by the National Education Association and by the state education associations, quickly reveals that in such publications any real disagreement on *fundamental* issues is never tolerated. This is true despite the fact that these organizations attempt to steer a middle course and have been labeled "conservative" by the more extreme progressives.

These journals give some space to the discussion of methodology and more to inspirational articles, but the articles which deal with educational philosophy are nearly always reaffirmations of faith. A teacher may read dozens of issues of such journals without finding a single article which questions the validity of pragmatic principles. And so complete and successful has been his indoctrination that he will probably be unable to see why this complete uniformity of thought is unhealthy. One who questions its desirability will be asked, "But what other points of view are there in education? Surely you do not want to go back to the old-style school with its emphasis on subject matter and its neglect of the needs of the growing child? Or are you a follower of Hutchins?"

This assumption that the neoscholasticism of the Chicago group is the only alternative to pragmatism reveals the philosophical bankruptcy of many teachers and other adults.

But it is true that the only *intellectual* criticism of progressive education which has recently come to the attention of any large number of people is that of Robert Maynard Hutchins and his associates, Adler, Buchanan, and Barr, whose views have been widely publicized in the popular magazines. Many of our countrymen have come to believe that the choice of an educational philosophy must lie between the views of these critics on the one hand and that of the pragmatists on the other. All other alternatives, and there are many, seem to have been ignored.

Unfortunately Dewey and Hutchins, although the clash of their basic philosophies is clear, never met in clear-cut opposition on educational issues. Dewey concerned himself largely with elementary and secondary education, while Hutchins is preoccupied with higher education; he is interested in the high school primarily as a preparation for the Hutchins conception of a college.

Some of Dewey's supporters have assumed that what is good for the child is equally appropriate for the youth of twenty, but it is by no means clear that Dewey himself made such an assumption. And Hutchins's views on elementary education are relatively unknown; probably he considers such education outside his bailiwick. It is interesting to note in passing that while the pragmatists and progressives talk enthusiastically about educating the "whole child" some neoscholastics seem equally enthusiastic about the "whole man." To a neutral observer it might seem that a whole man is just a whole child grown up. Of course, one very significant difference is that the pragmatists give the school full responsibility for all aspects of the child's development, while the neoscholastics would have the college limit its responsibilities largely to intellectual development, leaving vocational training, social development, and other functions to other agencies. In this conflict the teachers colleges have almost unanimously sided with Dewey.

If we are to continue the reexamination of first principles which has been proposed, it will be necessary that the colleges which prepare teachers for the public schools offer courses in which such reexamination is made. In a few colleges such courses are now available, but in a great many the only course offered in educational philosophy is one in which pragmatism is presented as the truth and in which other philosophies, if they are mentioned at all, are cited as examples of the errors of our benighted ancestors. If anyone doubts this, he need only question an unselected group of teachers on fundamental philosophical issues, or he may examine the textbooks used in some of these courses.

He will, to be sure, find a few textbooks which really do present a number of philosophical points of view and which discuss the implications of each for education. *Modern Philosophies of Education* by Professor John S. Brubacher of Yale is an excellent example, and there are others. But he will find that some of the more widely used texts on "philosophies of education" contain no philosophy at all; there is no search for first principles, only a reaffirmation of the progressive faith with suggestions for the application of this faith in the classroom.

Those who confuse indoctrination with philosophy may profitably read a few passages from the Inaugural Address of Charles W. Eliot, October 19, 1869 (as quoted in Commager, *Living Ideas in America*, Harper & Brothers, New York, 1951, p. 584). "Philosophical subjects should never be taught with authority. They are not established sciences; they are full of disputed matters, open questions, and bottomless speculations. It is not the function of the teacher to settle philosophical and political controversies for the pupil, or even to recommend to him any one set of opinions as better than another. Exposition, not imposition, of opinions is the professor's part. The student should be made acquainted with all sides of these controversies . . . the very word 'education' is a standing protest against dogmatic teaching. The notion that education consists in the authoritative inculcation of what the teacher deems true may be logical and appropriate in a convent, or a seminary for priests, but it is intolerable in universities and public schools from primary to professional." This is no less true in 1953 than it was in 1869.

But if we are to give our teachers freedom to examine the basic principles, it is not enough that the professors of educational philosophy play their part. It is equally important that those who supervise student teaching be willing to reexamine the basic assumptions which underly their practices and to allow such reexamination on the part of those who are undertaking their first teaching experience.

Somehow, a new freedom of inquiry must be brought into educational discussions. We must get away from the prevailing notion that anyone who raises questions about basic principles is antisocial, unprofessional, or reactionary. We must welcome criticism.

Space in the professional journals should be given to this reexamination of first principles, for there is need of a thoroughgoing exchange of ideas among those who have given most thought to these problems. There is in every teachers college a coterie of professors who are free from the current dogmatisms and clichés. Some of these individuals prefer the basic principles of pragmatism but wish to reexamine their implications for education. Others take serious intellectual exceptions to pragmatism and all its works and would like to explore the possibilities of basing an education for 1953 and the years ahead upon a different set of assumptions. And in the public schools there are a great many teachers who are both willing and able to take part in the discussion.

If these individuals cannot find a forum in the journals of the professional educational organizations, as it appears they cannot at present, perhaps they can find it in other educational publications. If these too are closed to anything which sounds to the editors like controversy, there are still the popular magazines and the journals of opinion. The editors of these journals welcome intelligent controversy, and publication in them has the additional advantage that through them it is possible for all members of the community who are interested in education to take part in the discussion.

It may well be that the figure of John Dewey will long continue to dominate the scene in American education. It is to be hoped that the figure will not become completely lost in the nebulous shadow which has come to obscure it. And let us hope that pragmatism will not continue its present course of ossification into a new dogmatism.

# CHAPTER IV

# WHAT IS PROGRESSIVE EDUCATION?

This chapter ought to begin with a simple, straightforward definition of progressive education. But in fact there is no such thing. What is called "progressive education" is nebulous, and it submits to no definition acceptable to all or even to a majority of those who account themselves progressive. Progressive education means very different things to different people; this is the source of much of the confusion.

Some have attempted to identify progressivism with all the modern trends in education. Carleton Washburne, a past president of the Progressive Education Association, says in his recent book *What Is Progressive Education?* that progressive education is simply an attempt to incorporate into current educational practice the latest advances of science. He explains that all professions lean heavily on the sciences, and just as medicine relies upon physiological research so education relies upon advances in psychology. It is true that there is and ought to be such a dependence, but Washburne's definition is far too simple. For some of the progressive trends are based upon new value judgments rather than upon research, and on the other hand there are a great many educators who are thoroughly familiar with psychological research who totally reject some of the viewpoints held by progressive educators.

Teachers themselves are confused and uncertain. If you were to ask one hundred teachers whether they accepted the principles of progressive education and followed these principles in their teaching, it is unlikely that you would get clear answers from half a dozen. Some would say that it depended upon what is meant by progressive education, but they would be much too cautious to offer a definition themselves. Some would reply, rather vaguely, that they are progressive but not with a capital "P." Many would counter by asking what *you* mean by "progressive."

Yet much of the current educational controversy has seemed to center around this nebulous set of theories or practices which floats like a wispy phantom in and out of the pages of recent educational history. "Seemed," because much of the controversy is based upon what is actually observed in the contemporary public schools, and the great majority of these schools are not and never have been progressive in any sense or to any degree that is even mildly satisfactory to those who call themselves progressives. It is worth noting that some of the most progressive schools are among those which are privately controlled, and it is the private school which has been extolled by some of those most critical of public education.

But if progressive education is a phantom, it is a very active and energetic one which is not easily laid to rest. Phantom or not, it continues to be denounced, ridiculed, and viewed with alarm. Anyone who criticizes it must expect to be roundly denounced in turn; he will probably be labeled a reactionary and an enemy of the schools. For "progressive" is still a fighting word even though its meaning is unclear. Perhaps one of the characteristics of fighting words is that they do not lend themselves to clear definition.

Progressive education began as a reform movement at a time

when some educational reforms were badly needed. It was a revolt against an intellectual tradition in education which some critics believed neglected the needs of the average child—a tradition which seemed to favor the development of an intellectual aristocracy. It was a revolt against a too severe discipline or perhaps against a tendency to confuse corporal punishment with discipline. It was a revolt against an earlier belief that the mind could profitably be trained by drill and by memorization. Such a revolt was probably necessary and desirable. But it is a characteristic of reform movements that they get carried away by their own exuberance and do not know when they have gone far enough. Long before they finally grind to a halt they split into warring sects, each of which makes dogmas out of some of the ideas which once seemed so fresh, so bright, so revolutionary.

All these things have happened to the educational movement which long called itself—and for a time really was—progressive. Not only has progressive education lost its momentum, it seems almost to have lost its identity.

In educational literature the term "progressive" appeared most frequently between the years 1925 and 1935. In recent years it has been used less and less even by those usually considered leaders of the movement. John Dewey, though he disclaimed the honor, is frequently looked upon as the father of progressivism and his name was always at the masthead of progressive publications. But Dewey rarely used the term in his later writings and, so far as I can discover, never defined it. At times he took sharp exception to educational practices which others called progressive.

In the course of his writings, Dewey criticized some of the progressives "for indulging pupils in unrestrained freedom of action and speech, of manners, and lack of manners," and said, "Ultimately it is the absence of intellectual control through significant subject matter which stimulates the deplorable egotism, cockiness, impertinence, and the disregard for the rights of others apparently considered by some persons to be the inevitable accompaniment, if not the essence of freedom" (*New Republic*, July 9, 1930).

This is very harsh criticism. Yet this is Dewey speaking, and he is speaking about some of the schools which called themselves progressive. It is obvious that progressive education cannot be adequately defined as the education of John Dewey. Dewey had a good deal to do with promoting the trend, but he became well aware that some of his ideas had gotten badly out of hand.

William Heard Kilpatrick of Teachers College, Columbia, has for thirty years or more been the outstanding exponent and popularizer of progressive education; he, more than any other one man, has come to be identified with it. But in 1951, when Kilpatrick summed up his ideas in *Philosophy of Education*, he did so without once using the term "progressive education." There is no attempt at a definition, unless the entire book is to be considered a definition; and it must be confessed that a definition of 450 pages is a little too long to be useful to us here.

Counts, Rugg, and many other leaders of progressivism have, at least in recent years, shown a reluctance to come to grips with the problem of definition. The very vagueness of the magic word is a source of its vitality. If it were sharply defined, it would be possible for those in disagreement to make a clear-cut assault. But no matter what line of attack the critics may take, the defenders can say with truth that they do not really understand what they are attacking.

If the critic objects to the idea of a child-centered school, the defender can object that the attack is unfair; he can quote Counts, a progressive, who said, "Progressive Education *cannot* place its trust in a child-centered school."

If the critic charges that progressives lean towards collectivism, the reply will be that some progressives favor almost unlimited individual freedom.

When the critic objects to the progressive dictum "education is not preparation for life—education *is* life," the reply is that *some* progressive schools include a good deal of vocational training which is surely preparation for adult life. Yet all these charges are true of some progressive schools and all the replies are true of others.

As of 1953, one can find hardly a single principle which is agreed upon by all who call themselves progressive. If he does find such a principle, he will discover that teachers who do not think of themselves as progressive are equally in agreement with it. Progressives make use of available information regarding the psychology of the child, but so do many of their opponents. Progressives want children to enjoy their school years, but so does nearly everyone else. Progressives believe in democracy, as do we all.

II

As things stand in 1953, progressive education is not so much a set of ideas or principles as it is an *attitude* toward education, an attitude highly charged with emotion or, perhaps more accurately, with sentiment.

The ideas and principles which once characterized progressivism no longer distinguish it clearly from other contemporary education. Some of the once-progressive ideas have been incorporated into all contemporary forms of education. Harsh discipline has become less common in nearly all schools. Intellectual standards have become more flexible or, to put it bluntly, have been lowered to meet the abilities of the less capable students. There is less drill in nearly all schools, with the possible exception of a few like those in New York, where the Regents' examinations are used and children are drilled in preparation for them. In all schools there has been a broadening of the curriculum to include just about everything under the sun, with consequently less emphasis on intellectual activities. Schools which are never considered progressive show these changes, for good or for ill, just about as much as do the progressive ones.

But progressive education as an attitude is still very much with us, particularly in the teachers colleges and the university colleges of education. In its more moderate forms this attitude is not particularly objectionable to most Americans, for it appears only as a rather self-conscious extroversion, an insistent optimism, and a love of change for the sake of change. Enthusiasm is preferred to criticism, action to ideas. Such attitudes are not confined to the schools but may be found up and down Main Street.

But in the most extreme progressives, in those who love to carry the progressive banner, there is also an evangelistic fervor, a spirit of rebellion against cold facts and closely reasoned logic, and a contempt for all that is old in education. Their favorite adjective is "old-fashioned," their most punishing is "reactionary." "Traditional" is always a term of reproach; "conservative" is not a description but an insult.

If you wish to be branded as conservative by a really progressive educator, you need only use such words as "fact," "subject matter," and "discipline." For he detests the word "fact" even though, when hard pressed, he may insist that his schools teach more facts than do other schools. He abhors the term "subject matter" and slays his opponents by describing them as "subject-matter-minded." "Discipline" is equally objectionable to him; he seems to suspect all who use the term of wanting to beat small children. His objection to these words is emotional rather than rational, as he may himself admit; for to him emotion is more important than reason. He finds these words repellent because they are identified in his thinking with the past—with the day when intellectualism dominated the schools, and children as growing individuals were neglected.

Progressivism in education is the high-water mark of the anti-intellectualism which has been developing in the Western world since Rousseau's revolt against the rationalism of his time. The agents of the eighteenth-century Enlightenment held that universal education would teach all men to think logically and that logical thinking would enable them to solve their problems. Truth could be discovered through reason and the truth would set us free. Rousseau, though he was a child of the Enlightenment, did not share the confidence of the rationalists that theirs was the road to a better world, and he became the first of the modern anti-intellectuals and the grandfather of progressive education.

The entire nineteenth century was a battleground between the rationalists and the antirationalists or anti-intellectualists who attacked from all sides. The romantic movement was essentially antirational, as were such divergent lines of attack as those of Marx, Nietzsche, Freud, and James. Despite their tremendous differences of opinion, these thinkers all held that the mainsprings of action are to be found not in man's reason but in his will or motives. And they held that will and motive are not controlled by intellect. To them action was more important than reason, and action was not dependent upon reason.

Yet throughout the nineteenth century the schools were controlled by the rationalists. Subject matter was organized on a rational, or logical, basis and the principal activities of the school were intellectual.

Progressive education had its beginnings in the revolt against this emphasis upon reason, and in its beginning had the support of the anti-intellectuals, who distrusted abstract deductive thinking. It was in the primary school that exclusively intellectual education was most vulnerable, and it was here that progressive education gained its foothold. But so long as progressivism limited itself to the kindergarten and the primary grades, there was not a great deal of opposition, for many were willing to admit that a purely intellectual approach to education had never made much sense in dealing with small children. The children seemed to be happier in the newer schools and, in many cases, seemed to learn as much as or more than they had in the older schools.

But by 1920 the progressives were demanding that their methods be used in the high schools, and this extension met with widespread opposition from teachers and parents alike. It led also to vigorous criticism from the few remaining rationalists.

The rationalist attacks had little real influence upon the more extreme progressives. Demonstrations of logical inconsistency did not greatly trouble them, since they had little confidence in logic as a road to truth. Their usual reply to a logical attack consisted in raising questions as to the critic's motives. Their anti-intellectualism was reflected in the kind of vague language in which the true progressive still revels. He likes to speak of "enriched experiences," of "on-going experiences," of the "emerging curriculum," and of "dynamic activities." Unfortunately, such pedaguese, though of progressive origins, has come to dominate a large part of the current educational literature. The fact that these phrases do not convey any very precise meaning does not seem to trouble the thoroughgoing progressive. They do convey the implication of action, and to him action is all important.

It must be clearly stated that I am speaking here about the philosophy or the attitude of progressive education as it appears in its more extreme form in textbooks, in progressive journals, and in the speeches at educational meetings which teachers are required to attend. Some of the schools which have been denoted progressive are very good schools by anyone's standards. This is particularly true of some of the school systems in the wealthier suburbs of the large cities. But these schools are good not primarily because of their progressive philosophy, which they calmly ignore when it serves their purposes. They are good because they have sufficient funds to attract the best teachers and to buy excellent buildings and equipment. They are good because they hire enough teachers so that classes are small and the teacher has an opportunity to give individual attention where individual attention is needed. In their actual philosophies many of these schools are no more progressive than are some of the very poor schools in poorer sections of the country.

Many teachers, unfamiliar with the actual philosophy of progressivism, are prone to approve of it because they have seen some good schools which are called progressive and many poor schools which are not called progressive. Many parents fall into the same fallacy.

III

The meaning of progressive education has not always been quite so vague as it seems today. Thirty years ago progressive education might have been defined as that education which was espoused by the Progressive Education Association.

This organization was founded in 1918. It grew to a membership of about 10,000 in the late 1930s, changed its name in 1944 to the American Education Fellowship, and has since declined to about half its maximum size. At no time did it include more than 1 per cent of all American teachers in its membership.

In its early years the P.E.A. laid great stress upon giving the child freedom to develop naturally, upon the importance of interest as a motivation for all work, and upon the role of the teacher as a guide and not a taskmaster. It stressed the all-round development of the child and consequently placed less emphasis upon purely intellectual activities. There was great emphasis upon the so-called "needs" of the child—a teleological concept which was never very clearly defined and which probably does not lend itself to definition.

But these principles gave slight indication of the directions which the several varieties of progressive education were to take. For by 1934 the movement had split into many warring factions, some of which professed totally incompatible views. In 1936 Pedro T. Orata, in *Educational Administration and Supervision* (Vol. 22, pp. 361–374, 1936), published an article with the arresting subtitle "Fifty-seven Varieties of Progressive Education." Orata recognized three main varieties, but it appears to me that there were actually four: (1) The conservative wing, which advocated the use of progressive methods in the teaching of conventional subject matter; (2) the close followers of John Dewey; (3) the reconstruction-of-the-social-order variety; and (4) the do-as-you-please variety or lunatic fringe, which advocated complete freedom of self-expression for children, virtually without adult control.

The criticisms of progressive education have rarely been based upon those who used progressive methods in the teaching of subject matter. Good teachers have always revised their methods pretty continuously, adjusting them to changing conditions. They welcome the suggestions of the newer educators regarding new methods of teaching.

The second group of progressives, the true Deweyites, de-emphasized subject matter and placed major stress upon the process of growth. They denied that education should be thought of as preparation for adult life. This is a logical consequence of following the philosophy of instrumentalism; Dewey said, "There is nothing to which growth is relative save more growth; there is nothing to which education is subordinate save more education." And again, "Since growth is the characteristic of life, education is all one with growing; it has no end beyond itself." (John Dewey, *Democracy and Education*, pp. 60–62.) This main stream of progressivism gave rise to the activity movement and to the project method. Although its principles met with serious objection from philosophers, they were largely accepted by leaders in education, and had some influence upon all the public schools—though the influence was not clear-cut and often resulted in confusion.

The *public* criticism of the progressive movement was based to a great extent upon the two remaining varieties of progressivism, varieties which did not logically follow from Dewey's philosophy and to which Dewey himself took vigorous exception.

One small group of educators proposed that teachers should take the lead in reconstructing the social order, and that the direction of social change should be determined by the educators themselves. (I wish to emphasize the smallness of this group and to point out that they were mostly professors rather than classroom teachers in the public schools. This group included only a small proportion of all progressives, but they were identified as progressives and they received much more attention than their numbers warranted.) There were two very serious objections to these proposals: first, the objection to allowing any one professional group to determine the direction of social change; and second, a conviction on the part of many who read the proposals that these progressives were demanding social changes which would lead to collectivism and perhaps to a totalitarian government. The group called upon the teachers of the nation to "recognize the corporate and the interdependent character of the contemporary order, and transfer the democratic tradition from individualistic to collectivist foundations" (John Day Pamphlets, No. 50, The John Day Company, New York, 1935, p. 21). They denied that they were proposing anything other than true democracy, because they insisted that collectivism and democracy were fully compatible; but it was their proposals which convinced many citizens that progressive education had socialistic or even communistic leanings.

Finally, it was what Orata called the "let freedom ring" boys who made possible most of the jokes about progressive education, such as the classic in which the wistful little girl asks, "Teacher, do we *have* to do whatever we want to again today?" (It seems that there really were a few schools in which children were allowed to do almost exactly as they pleased.)

This lunatic fringe, also a small but vocal group, took an elaborately sentimental attitude toward children. Children, the little darlings, are closer to nature than adults and hence are nobler, finer, more sensitive, and purer of spirit. This attitude would have delighted Rousseau, disgusted Hobbes, and amused Aristotle. One who was neither delighted nor amused was John Dewey. As early as 1930 he felt it necessary to criticize the more extreme progressives for carrying "the thing called freedom nearly to the point of anarchy" ( New Republic, July 9, 1930). Dewey made it clear that in his opinion some adult control and direction are necessary in the proper education of children, for he said, "To fail to assure them guidance and direction is not merely to permit them to operate in a blind and spasmodic fashion, but it promotes the formation of habits of immature, undeveloped and egoistic activity."

It may reasonably be said that *some* of those who recently have criticized the schools are closer to the principles of John Dewey than some who call themselves progressive.

IV

This new education, which began in a spirit of rebellion against dogmas and against practices which had become sterile, has in less than fifty years developed dogmas of its own and come to be resentful of criticism. To those familiar with the history of ideas it will not be surprising that those who hold to the newer tenets indignantly deny that they are dogmas, but insist rather that they are "truths."

The most pervasive of these "truths" is that pragmatism, sometimes in the newer forms of instrumentalism and experimentalism, has finally replaced all earlier philosophical systems. Of course very few teachers have any clear understanding of the subtleties of pragmatic philosophy, but the belief that other philosophies are obsolete is widespread. A natural consequence has been that when educational practices are criticized by those possessing some knowledge of philosophy—by Robert Maynard Hutchins, by Mortimer Smith, by Bernard Iddings Bell—the teachers are unable to defend their practices intelligently. They tend to fall back on clichés and educational gobbledygook, which merely convinces critics of the intellectual sterility of the educational profession.

Despite this confusion, some of the newer trends in education have led to, or have been contemporary with, very real improvements in the schools. Only a scattered few nostalgic elder citizens really would like to go back to the education of

1900. Education has blundered its way forward with many a twist and turn, but forward nonetheless. Despite the confusion of psychological systems, we know a great deal more about the motivation and the learning processes of children than we did a half century ago, and some of this knowledge has found its way into the classroom.

The present confusion results in part from the absence of effective leadership; never before in the memory of living teachers has there been so conspicuous a lack of it in educational thought. A generation ago, when Dewey and Bode were providing vigorous leadership on the philosophical level, Thorndike and Judd were rigorously investigating the psychology of learning and providing a scientific basis for new methods of teaching. The new education was being popularized and promoted by Kilpatrick; Bagley provided effective criticism of the newer trends.

But of these giants of the first half century, Dewey, Thorndike, Judd, Bagley, and now Bode are no longer with us. Kilpatrick is eighty-two. No one has come to take their places. The minor leaders of progressivism, the spokesmen of today, are busy battling off critics who attack from all sides. They persistently make the mistake of trying to lump all their opponents together and to stifle them with cries of "reactionary." In their present defensive position they are totally unable to provide the aggressive and intelligent leadership needed in planning for the schools of tomorrow.

The progressives of today devote far too large a part of their energies to attacks upon medievalism, upon Alexandrianism, upon the Ichabod Cranes and the Hoosier Schoolmasters of the past. They fail to see that at least a portion of today's criticism is based not upon a wish to return to the past but upon a clearer vision of the future: American education in 1953 is evolving not *toward* progressive education but *past* it.

In 1938 John Dewey foresaw that "an educational philosophy which professes to be based on the idea of freedom may become as dogmatic as ever was the traditional education which it reacted against. For any theory and set of practices is dogmatic which is not based upon critical examination of its own underlying principles" (*Experience and Education*, p. 10). Dewey was reacting to some of the things which even fifteen years ago were beginning to be apparent. Now, in 1953, it seems clear that his prediction has been fulfilled. Progressive education, or the fragment of it which still exists as a specific movement, has come to resent all criticism of itself and to accept its own diluted form of pragmatism as dogma, while ceasing to give critical examination to its underlying principles. It has left us with many valuable legacies but also with a great deal of confusion. It has at times led us down strange byways. No longer does it point the way.

It is to be hoped that we can find the way ahead without jettisoning the very real accomplishments of the past half century. I am convinced that we can. But progressive education and progress in education no longer are synonymous—if, indeed, they ever were.

# CHAPTER V

# THE MAN OF STRAW

In some of the more odious of the recent attacks upon school policies much use has been made of the straw-man technique. The straw man which is set up is the critic's conception of a progressive school, and to it have been ascribed all the extreme and bizarre characteristics ever attributed to any modern educational institution. Such a man of straw is easily and effectively assailed.

The teacher is well aware that no one school has ever embodied all these ridiculous practices, and that some of them have rarely if ever been found in any school. Naturally he feels that the technique used in the attack is intellectually dishonest or at best based upon misinformation.

In this the teacher is quite correct; but the straw-man technique should not be unfamiliar to him. For he himself—or at any rate those who taught him—has been using it very effectively for a long time.

The straw man which the educators have set up for their target is the school of the past or, more precisely, the teacher of the past. It is never very clear just when or where this teacher existed, but he has been described in great detail in many books on "the new education," by lecturers at numerous education conferences, and in a goodly number of courses in education. Every teacher will recognize him easily.

This teacher of the past seems to be a cross between Ichabod Crane and the Hoosier Schoolmaster. He is not very bright but has, curiously enough, some of the intellectual assurance of a Mortimer Adler. In addition, he is dogmatic, sadistic, arrogant, and preoccupied with petty facts. He hates children and would dispense with them entirely if he could do so and still keep his job.

The school over which he presides is one in which the children sit in straight rows stiffly at attention and speak only when spoken to. When they do speak it is only to recite facts memorized from a horrible document called a textbook. All natural tendencies of the child are inhibited or ruthlessly suppressed and joy is forbidden. A birch rod hangs in the corner and is frequently used for emphasis, for Ichabod is convinced that the road to the mind is through the seat of the pants.

In contrast to this iniquitous institution the speaker at our education conference, or the writer of the book on the new schools, or the professor of education presents in glowing terms the progressive school of our enlightened present day. Here all is sweetness and light. Children sit in a semicircle in chairs which are not attached to the floor and which can thus be dragged easily across the floor to the accompaniment of those sweet scraping sounds so dear to the ears of the growing child. There are no textbooks; there is no memorization. Of course the children really learn more facts than did their grandparents—the eight-year study proves that—but all this is accomplished incidentally and painlessly.

In this new school the child does not learn, he "grows"; he unfolds like a lovely flower on a summer day revealing all the richness and beauty that is within him.

When he misbehaves it is in no sense his fault but the fault of a wayward society or perhaps the fault of his parents who have failed to prepare him for the new freedom.

So much for the straw-man technique. Critics of the school have used it, educators have used it, and I have made just a tiny bit of use of it in this chapter. It is an effective and often entertaining technique, but it is not a very effective means of discovering the truth, for it obscures more often than it clarifies.

If, in making our plans for the school of the future, we wish to make a comparison of the school of yesterday with the school of today, we had better toss out the straw men and do the best we can to examine the facts.

How much truth is there to the educator's conception of the school of bygone years? No doubt there were a few Ichabods; Hoosier Schoolmasters turned up here and there, and there was—and is—Mortimer Adler. But there was also my Aunt Lena.

Aunt Lena, now a very elderly lady, began teaching school as a teen-age girl back in the eighties. She never had a course in education; she had married and had left the profession long before anyone had heard of the new education. But Aunt Lena, besides being highly intelligent, was a very kindly lady who loved children. That they loved her in return was demonstrated by the fact that in her later years her former pupils often came to see her and to tell her how happily they remembered the years spent in her school and how much they learned from her.

In her school they learned the three R's, but certainly the learning was not limited to that. They read and talked about the Constitution and the Declaration of Independence. They discussed values. They did not think of it as a study of values, but no one can read and discuss the McGuffey *Readers* without considering values.

At recess they played gaily, and she played with them. In her classroom the benches were fastened to the floor and were arranged in straight rows but there was no rigidity about the thinking.

Those of our older citizens who were fortunate enough to have attended schools presided over by the Aunt Lenas rather than by the Ichabods sometimes express a nostalgic yearning to return to the old days, and occasionally one of these elders goes so far as to suggest that all our educational problems might be solved by such a return. This is a pleasant thought, for it seems so simple a solution, but we would do well not to let our nostalgia get the better of us. The educational problems of today cannot be solved by a return to the little red schoolhouse.

## II

No writer on the subject of education has used the straw-man technique so frequently and so effectively as has William Heard Kilpatrick. The skillful use of this technique is one of the keys to Kilpatrick's tremendous influence.

Dr. Kilpatrick, now professor emeritus of Teachers College, Columbia, has long been the leading spokesman for progressivism. Though less profound than Dewey, he writes far more clearly and is much more effective as a lecturer.

In his recently published *Philosophy of Education*, Kilpatrick uses this technique throughout the book but demonstrates it most skillfully in Chapter XVI in which he compares the "Old" concept of education, which he calls the "Alexandrian," with the "New," *i.e.*, the Kilpatrick concept.

The "Old" concept is a composite straw man made up of a hodgepodge of educational theories, practices, and institutions including the medieval university, catechismal schools, the Boston Latin School, the New York Regents' examination system, the humanistic tradition, and practically all contemporary high schools and colleges except those few which are conspicuously progressive. These are strange bedfellows. Still stranger is the presence among them of Robert Maynard Hutchins and Mark Van Doren.

Kilpatrick tries, not very convincingly, to trace the roots of all these divergent trends back to the Egyptian education which developed in the city of Alexandria shortly after the death of Alexander the Great in 323 B.C.

According to Kilpatrick this "Old" concept of education places its reliance on memory in "the cold-storage sense." It stresses catechizing and the use of harsh physical punishments to assure blind obedience. It devotes itself to the cultivation of the intellect and completely ignores both character and body building. It insists upon a classroom consisting of rows of seats which are screwed to the floors.

Professor Kilpatrick now calls upon all those who wish to devote themselves to the "Old" education to stand up and show themselves. The clear implication is that all who do not jump to their feet are progressives whether or not they are aware of it.

But it seems only fair that we should be allowed to ask a few questions at this point: Can Dr. Kilpatrick really believe that the medieval university gave no thought to the development of character? Can he honestly say that the contemporary liberal arts college which follows the humanistic tradition insists upon blind obedience? Would Hutchins and Van Doren approve a catechismal school in which students were not allowed to do their own thinking? Does Notre Dame University, which is surely not a progressive school, ignore muscle building?

The straw man is apparent. There is no "Old" education in the sense that Kilpatrick has described it. There are many old concepts of education and many new concepts. It is entirely possible to reject *in toto* the Alexandrian concept and to reject simultaneously the concept of the progressives.

We are reminded of an evangelist who describes the devil in vivid language and then asks all followers of Satan to stand up and be counted. The others are left with no choice but to join the church of the evangelist. But some of us believe there may be other roads which lead to salvation.

# CHAPTER VI

# THE TEACHERS COLLEGE IN AMERICA

If all institutions of higher learning were ranked in terms of prestige, it seems likely that the teachers college would find itself low man on the educational totem pole. Yet this much-maligned and frequently ridiculed institution probably exerts more influence upon the American scene than does any other type of college; for if the graduate of the teachers college is badly educated, the children in the public schools, and eventually the American people, will be badly educated. And there is reason to question whether a nation of badly educated men and women can permanently maintain its free institutions.

If liberally educated and thoughtful Americans are dubious about the way in which the teachers college is doing its work, it is not enough that they regard it with scorn. They must examine it carefully; they must become familiar with the facts —not with the facts of 1920 but with the facts of 1953—and with the direction being taken, which will tell something of the teachers college of the future.

The facts are somewhat obscured by the substantial differences which exist among the teachers colleges in the various states and the equally great differences which exist among liberal arts colleges. The observer or the critic is likely to form his generalizations on the basis of the teachers colleges as he sees them in his own section of the country. A conspicuous example of this fallacy was found in the widely read article "Who Teaches the Teachers" under the pseudonym of John William Sperry, which appeared in *Life*'s famous education issue of October 16, 1950.

Mr. Sperry says, "Teachers' Colleges usually do not have equipment, buildings, or campuses comparable to those of liberal arts colleges or universities. Several teachers' colleges I saw looked more like grammar schools than colleges . . . a great many of the teachers' colleges bring an inferior faculty and an inferior student body together in an inferior physical plant." And farther on in the article Mr. Sperry makes the flat statement, "All were distinctly inferior to *every* liberal arts college or university I have ever seen." (The italics are mine.)

Now this covers a lot of ground—or perhaps it suggests that Mr. Sperry had *not* covered much ground. It appears that he formed his judgments on the basis of a few colleges on the East Coast. He does say that he had visited some teachers colleges in the Middle West and the South, but one is forced to conclude that he thinks of western Pennsylvania as the Middle West, for surely he did not get as far as Ohio where he would have found that the state teachers colleges—now called universities—at Bowling Green and Kent have physical plants far superior to those of most of the numerous private liberal arts colleges in that state.

The American teachers college is, in its most important development, a phenomenon of the Middle West and the Far West. Along the Eastern seaboard, where the liberal arts college was well entrenched before the teachers college got its start, the newer institution has in many states remained a neglected school with inadequate facilities, downtrodden faculties, a student body consisting all too often of those who could not gain admittance to the more selective colleges of liberal arts.

But west of the Alleghenies the teachers college is frequently a very different type of institution, and so, in many cases, is the college of liberal arts.

What is a teachers college? At first glance it might seem obvious that a teachers college is any college which prepares teachers. But what are we to say when we find that there are a great many so-called "liberal arts" colleges half or more of whose graduates enter the teaching profession and when we find many institutions called teachers colleges, fewer than half of whose students have any intention of entering that profession? Many of our state teachers colleges offer a liberal arts course or a general education course for those who prefer not to become teachers and the number is increasing yearly.

The student who does plan to teach finds that the course of study laid out for him is very much the same whether he enrolls in an institution calling itself a liberal arts college or one which is called a teachers college. In either case about three-fourths of his work will be in academic areas, including English, social studies, natural sciences, and fine arts. The other one-fourth will consist of courses in the philosophy and the methodology of education and in practice teaching. If he plans to become a high-school teacher, the proportion of his time devoted to academic work will be somewhat higher regardless of the type of institution in which he enrolls, and if he plans to teach in the lower grades a larger part of his time will be devoted to methods and to practice teaching. If he happens to study in one of the few states which have the General Certificate—the certificate which purports to represent preparation for teaching at all levels—there will be no such distinction.

The fact is that in those states west of Pennsylvania the

difference between the teachers college and the college of liberal arts has all but disappeared. The proof of this statement does not require an elaborate survey. It is true that an accurate evaluation of the true merits of any college is difficult if not impossible, but the kind of superficial facts about physical plants mentioned in Mr. Sperry's article can be gathered for all colleges without moving out of one's library. An excellent source is the volume *American Colleges and Universities*, published by the American Council on Education. Let us take a look at some of the measurable facts as given in the latest edition published in 1952.

I begin by looking up the facts of my own college, Western Washington College of Education in Bellingham, Washington. I find that the plant and equipment are valued at eight million dollars. This figure exceeds that given for such well-known liberal arts colleges as Amherst, Colgate, Hamilton, Barnard, Swarthmore, Antioch, and Santa Clara, each of which is comparable to the Bellingham institution in enrollment.

And Western Washington's facilities are not greatly different from those found at many other colleges of education throughout the states from Ohio westward. The State Teachers College at Terre Haute, Indiana, has a plant valued at ten million dollars. There are dozens of liberal arts colleges with equipment valued at less than one-tenth that amount. Iowa State Teachers College at Cedar Falls has a plant valued at six million, Michigan State Normal College at Ypsilanti over eleven million, and there are comparable plants in teachers colleges from Michigan to California. But these figures should be adequate to establish the fact that the inferiority of the teachers college, if such inferiority exists, cannot be attributed to poor buildings and facilities.

Faculties are another matter—and obviously the most important matter in judging the quality of a college. Unfortunately there is no satisfactory measure of the quality of a faculty. We can count doctoral degrees, academic honors, and publications, but no one believes that these are a completely valid index of quality of teaching.

Mr. Sperry, in his effort to evaluate the teaching in teachers colleges, rather naïvely resorted to the technique of asking the opinion of professors at liberal arts colleges. This is naïve because it overlooks the unhappy fact that the two types of institutions are currently engaged in a bitter competition for public support and for the more able students. Asking an Amherst professor for his opinion of a teachers college professor is roughly comparable to asking a Marine Corps colonel for his opinion of the faculty at West Point.

It seems reasonable to assume that in the long run the most able college teachers will find their way to those colleges which offer the greatest rewards. The rewards sought by American college professors are of many kinds; they include such things as prestige, the opportunity to live in a community of scholars where the interchange of ideas and the battle of wits will stimulate continued intellectual growth, the opportunity to work with able students, intellectual freedom, and, by no means least, the opportunity to enjoy the advantages of living in the world's wealthiest nation. These advantages are not fully available to one living on a minimum income, and so the professor, for all his interest in ideas, is concerned just as is the engineer, the physician, the clerk, or the shoemaker with increasing his income. Other things being equal he will, in time, find his way to the college which pays the best salary for his services.

The colleges which compete most vigorously for the professors who are teachers rather than research experts are the small liberal arts colleges and the teachers colleges. How well able are the teachers colleges to meet the competition?

It is not true that the average salaries paid to faculty members of teachers colleges throughout the United States are lower than the average paid by liberal arts colleges if we exclude a dozen private liberal arts colleges having exceptional endowments. A college, whether it be a teachers college or a college of liberal arts, can, in 1953, secure the services of a reasonably competent young teacher for four or five thousand dollars. For ten thousand a year it can get the very best professor available, not a nonteaching celebrity such as is sometimes used as window dressing by the private college but a real teacher, broad in outlook, brilliant, scholarly, skillful at making difficult ideas understandable, and capable of providing the human environment in which a confused adolescent can grow into an intellectually and emotionally mature adult.

A ten-thousand-dollar salary may not seem excessive to the businessman or to the man who has succeeded in another profession, but there is not a single teachers college in the United States, other than the graduate schools attached to universities, which offers such a salary to even its greatest teacher. The reason is not hard to find. A college will receive only minor criticism and much admiration for spending an extra hundred thousand dollars for nonfunctional Gothic decorations for the library, while it will receive far more criticism than approval if it spends one-tenth that amount for a professor's salary. A good building is impressive. A good professor usually looks pretty unimpressive to the average citizen.

The remarkable fact is that some superb teachers remain on the faculties of the teachers colleges despite the salaries. Thousands of teachers in Ohio will agree that the late Clayton C. Kohl of Bowling Green State Normal (now Bowling Green State University) was such a man. Only students have any real basis for judging a teacher, and I speak as one of Dr. Kohl's students. Though I have since attended some famous universities, I have known no one who could compare with Kohl as a teacher. So far as I know he never wrote a book. His skills were those of imparting great ideas orally, and he devoted all his time to teaching and to preparing himself to teach. His influence, through the thousands of teachers whom he taught, has left its mark on more than a full generation of Ohio school children and adolescents. Certainly his influence in northern Ohio was far greater than that of any physician, lawyer, or engineer in that area. I doubt if his salary ever exceeded six or seven thousand dollars a year. It is no exaggeration to say that he was worth a million.

But for every Kohl there are dozens of potential Kohls who are more ambitious for the things money can buy. They teach briefly in a small college and then move on to more remunerative work. Within recent years many of them have gone into the various types of government work available to academic people. If they join a university staff, they quickly find that it is writing and not teaching that pays. In an effort to gain promotion they neglect their teaching and become second-rate writers of semischolarly tomes and unread journal articles.

So it may well be true, as Mr. Sperry suggests, that the poor faculties which he reports finding in many of the teachers colleges are in part the result of inadequate salaries. But when a teachers college professor leaves his position for one which is better paid, he moves, in most cases, not to a liberal arts college but to a state college or state university. In many a western state the teachers colleges can successfully compete with salaries paid by private colleges, but their salaries are still distinctly lower than those paid to professors of engineering, law, agriculture, and dentistry at the state university. The citizen who wishes to improve the teachers colleges and who pays all the salaries through taxation may reasonably ask why.

If your state legislature provides, as it almost certainly does, higher salaries for the professor of animal husbandry at the state agricultural college than for the professor in the teachers college, it appears that the pedigreed bull is held in higher regard than is the human child. Such a contemptuous attitude toward children and toward their teachers may reasonably make the teacher cynical about the citizens' groups which profess to have as their aim the advancement of the schools, for I have yet to hear of any such group which has called the attention of the legislatures to this discrepancy.

Even if we are to conclude that the physical plants of our teachers colleges are already good in many sections of the country and are rapidly improving elsewhere, and if we are to conclude that the salaries are at least as good as those paid by many small private colleges, it by no means follows that all is well with the colleges of education. They have some very serious deficiencies, weaknesses which are all the more serious because they are not apparent to the casual observer and cannot be detected through the reading of catalogues or the blue book of colleges.

II

The teachers college—and this is true whether it exists as a separate institution or as part of a university—is in all too many cases a house divided against itself. On the one hand is the teacher-training division which supervises the practice teaching and which may or may not include the department of education—usually it does. On the other hand is the group of departments which is primarily concerned with what the first division scornfully refers to as "subject matter."

An outsider might reasonably expect to find these two groups working in harmony. He might expect that those who deal with the skills, the techniques, and the procedures of teaching would feel great need for subject-matter departments and that the academic departments would understand the need for and recognize the importance of the aspects of teacher education with which the other group is most concerned. But anyone who has taught in a college of education or has been a student in such a college can report that such an expectation is naïve, to say the least.

Almost any academic professor will tell you, if you promise not to quote him, that those in the teacher training division are trying to run the school, that they demand far too large a portion of the curriculum for themselves, that they waste too much time in needless repetition of educational clichés; if he gets really warmed up—as he probably will—he will add that the "educators" are intellectually inferior anyway.

The director of teacher training, or any member of his staff, is likely to say, again with assurance that he will not be quoted, that his biggest problem is the "subject-matter mindedness" of the academic professors. He will assure you that they know nothing of the realities of dealing with children and with practical school problems, that they consider facts more important than children, that they allow far too little room in the curriculum for practice teaching and for the learning of educational procedures; if he gets really warmed up—as he undoubtedly will—he will state that the "academicians" are a lot of vague theorists and stuffed shirts.

Viewed at a distance this schism is so fantastic as to be humorous, but from the standpoint of the student learning to become a teacher it is tragic. It leaves the student torn, confused, and troubled. It very seriously interferes with the proper functioning of the college. And this schism is even worse in the university or the liberal arts college which has a department of education than it is in the separate teachers college.

In fairness it should be said that there are a few teachers colleges in which this problem has been reduced somewhat in recent years, largely by the selection, over a period of time, of faculty members from both sides of the barrier who are sufficiently broad in their understandings to avoid such pettiness and who are sufficiently self-confident to avoid the defensiveness which has led to the schism. But for each such institution there are a dozen in which the two groups are almost incapable of talking the same language professionally.

The schism which we have been discussing is based, in part, upon a fundamental conflict of philosophies. Many of our professors in the academic departments have come through liberal arts colleges and graduate schools of the large universities. The large university, and this is particularly true of the state university, usually holds to no consistent philosophy; often different philosophical assumptions are made by each department. The small liberal arts college frequently bases its teaching upon a firmer and more consistent philosophic foundation. In some schools this foundation is frankly theological, the theology being that of the church which supports the college. In many other private colleges, less closely associated with a specific religious denomination, the philosophical basis is some variety of idealism, often with a humanistic bent.

In sharp contrast, the philosophy of the teachers colleges has come almost exclusively to be the type of pragmatism which Dewey calls instrumentalism or experimentalism. These schools base their procedures upon the assumptions that pragmatism has replaced other philosophies, that all other philosophies are outmoded. Yet such assumptions are totally unacceptable to the graduates of most liberal arts colleges and to a very considerable proportion of informed people everywhere.

Liberal arts graduates usually hold that education is a means to an end, though they may not entirely agree among themselves as to just what the ends are. But at least they will agree that mastery of subject matter is important.

Educators, on the contrary, agree with Dewey that "the educational process has no end beyond itself; it is its own end." "There is nothing to which growth is relative save more growth, there is nothing to which education is subordinate save more education," and further "education is all one with growing; it has no end beyond itself" (*Democracy and Education*, The Macmillan Company, New York, 1916, pp. 59–62).

Moreover the philosophy of the teachers college as represented by the educators is that education is a total process and that the schools must accept the major responsibility for this process. The school must concern itself with the child's health, his recreation, his character, his citizenship, his emotional development, his social adjustment, his vocational training, and his intellectual development. The teachers college is unwilling to concede that any one of these concerns is more important than the others because it considers any separation to be impossible. This point of view is consistent with and an outgrowth of the philosophy of pragmatism.

The attitude toward teaching which is held by the liberal arts college, on the other hand, was well stated by Charles A. Beard (writing in *School and Society*, Vol. 43, pp. 278–279, Feb. 29, 1936):

"The teacher is not a physician, a nurse, a soldier, a policeman, a politician, a businessman, a farmer, or an industrial worker. . . . The teacher's principle business is the training of minds and the dissemination of knowledge . . . the teacher is another kind of person with other duties and other responsibilities—the duty and responsibilities of the scholar."

It is obvious that these two conceptions of the role of the teachers are totally at variance, and there appears to be no real compromise or mid-point between them. Yet in most of the schools which prepare teachers half the faculty holds firmly to one point of view while the other half holds with equal firmness to the other. It is small wonder that the teacher graduating from such a college is confused.

### III

Though no immediate solution to this conflict is apparent the explanation for the schism may be found in the history of teacher education.

Prior to about 1920, high-school teachers and teachers for the elementary school were rarely educated in the same institutions. Most high schools recruited their teachers from universities or liberal arts colleges while the elementary teachers came from the normal schools.

The normal schools had their origin in New England. A private normal was opened at Concord, Vermont, in 1823, but it was Massachusetts which in 1839 established the first state-supported normal school at Lexington. Similar institutions were established in Connecticut in 1850 and in Rhode Island in 1852. Several Middle Western states followed suit prior to the Civil War, and after the war the movement spread rapidly until 1900 when all but a very few of the states in the Union were maintaining state normal schools. But these early normal schools bore little resemblance to anything which can properly be called higher education. Most of them accepted students directly from the elementary schools, and they were essentially high schools with some added work of a more or less professional nature.

After 1900, normal schools gradually increased their entrance requirements, for with the growth of public high schools it was no longer necessary for the normal school to provide secondary instruction. But as recently as 1920—and in many states much more recently—the commonly accepted standard for elementary teachers was one or two years of normal school beyond high school, and a great many rural and village teachers entered the profession with one summer term of normal-school preparation.

It is obvious that even during the early years of the present century these normal schools were not colleges. Most of them offered little or no subject matter at a college level. Their courses were of a so-called "practical" nature. Catalogues listed such subjects as School Management and Discipline, School Hygiene, Child Study, and Practical Pedagogy. Such academic work as was included was designed to reinforce the prospective teachers' knowledge of elementary-school subjects. Consequently the normal schools were in no way qualified to prepare teachers for the high schools or academies.

The development of the normal school into a teachers college or a college of education occurred during the period from about 1925 to 1940, and it was not until that period that the state normal began seriously to compete with the private liberal arts college in the preparation of teachers for secondary schools.

When the state normal schools were first established they gave no thought to the training of teachers for the high schools for the obvious reason that there were almost no high schools. There were, to be sure, academies or prep schools but these were preoccupied with the preparation of students for the colleges, usually one specific college, and it seemed natural that a school which prepared for, let us say, Princeton should get its faculty from among the graduates of that college.

But with the development of the public high school which followed the Civil War and continued at a much faster pace after the turn of the century, the preparation of high-school teachers became of paramount importance. Though a liberal arts degree was considered the proper preparation for teachers in secondary schools, many high-school administrators felt that their teachers could profit from some courses in pedagogy, and a few colleges and universities gave thought to the problem.

A chair in the philosophy of education had been established at the University of the City of New York (now New York University) in 1832. In 1853 the subject of pedagogy was introduced at Antioch College by Horace Mann, and by 1880 several other colleges and universities had followed suit. The movement spread rapidly, and by 1900 some 200 colleges and universities included education among their offerings.

But it would be erroneous to assume that pedagogy, or education as it came to be called, was accepted as a legitimate subject of study at the college level. The prevailing opinion was that teaching called for no special preparation, that the teacher needed only to know his subject thoroughly and to have a modicum of common sense. The professor of pedagogy was looked upon by his academic peers as an excrescence on the face of the community of scholars. He was scorned, humiliated, and ridiculed. In some institutions only a few daring students risked taking his elective courses, and the makers of collegiate curriculums rarely required such courses even of those who were planning to teach. In many colleges and universities more than a trace of this attitude persists to the present day. If those professional educators who have recently come to positions of great power occasionally show a touch of arrogance toward their academic associates, their attitude may be only a very natural compensation for their earlier humiliations.

The position of the professional educator in the normal school was very different from that of his brother in the college or university; in the normal school his field was considered to be one of prime importance. It was natural that many of the most competent teachers of education courses found their way to the normal schools rather than to the universities.

Though a few teachers colleges came into existence prior to World War I, the development of the normal school into the teachers college has, in most states, been a phenomenon of the past thirty years. During the 1920s normal schools in several states changed their names to teachers colleges or colleges of education, extended their courses to four years, and began granting college degrees. The movement spread during the succeeding two decades until by 1950 the state normal school had all but become a thing of the past. It is a curious commentary that in many a community this change seems to have come about without much public awareness; one frequently hears these schools referred to as "the normal" even in cities in which there has been no normal school for twenty years.

The change has by no means been in name only because the teachers college of 1953 bears little resemblance to the normal school of 1920. The faculty of the normal school of thirty years ago consisted largely of the more successful teachers and county superintendents of the region who had been called in to instruct prospective teachers. Some of the faculty members were college graduates, but many were graduates of other normal schools and held no college degrees. Only a very few had completed any graduate work in a university, and a doctoral degree was so rare as to be a subject for comment. Today the picture is very different. All, or very nearly all, of the present-day faculty members hold masters' degrees, and from one-fourth to one-third, in a few cases as many as one-half, hold doctoral degrees.

The subject matter taught consisted largely of educational methods, educational philosophy and history, a few lower-level college courses, and a review of the elementary subjects. Handwriting and spelling were commonly included among the offerings.

The teachers college of today offers a full four-year sequence of collegiate courses. Strictly professional courses usually account for about one-fourth of the curriculum, but all the other offerings are so nearly identical with those found in liberal arts colleges and universities that a student usually experiences no difficulty in transferring to such a school without loss of credit.

In a great many cases the teachers college of 1953 offers a general or liberal arts degree, and many offer the master's degree in education as well.

This extraordinarily rapid development of the normal school into the teachers college has not been accomplished without difficulty, confusion, and turmoil. If the teachers college has become a house divided against itself, as has been suggested, the division has been a consequence of rapid expansion and the resultant appointment of faculty members who propounded conflicting educational philosophies. For as the normal school became a college it became necessary for it to add to its academic staff. The county superintendents and experienced elementary teachers who made up its faculty in 1920 were not prepared to teach collegiate courses at the upper-division level, nor in many cases were they interested in doing so. A few of them hied themselves to the universities for additional graduate work. Those who did went most often to Columbia's Teachers College, for it was this institution which was most sympathetic with their problems. It was this institution also which offered masters' degrees without the formal requirement of oral examinations or a thesis, and it was these hurdles which were most awesome or which seemed most unreasonable to the older normal-school instructors, who after years of teaching elementary subjects found it necessary to compete with younger graduate students. Moreover Columbia's Teachers College had a way of convincing you that you really learned more about teaching within its halls than you would have learned in a graduate school with the customary graduate degree requirements. Here the student could sit at the feet of Dewey, Kilpatrick, and a host of lesser celebrities. Perhaps not quite at their feet because the class might number four or five hundred and you might find yourself in the back row where you could see little and hear less, but at least you could say you had had a course from the great men while others had only read their books.

So teachers from the normal schools came to Columbia by the thousands. Even so there were not enough to fill the swelling faculties of the new teachers colleges, particularly in the academic fields.

These teachers had to be recruited from other graduate schools. Many of these newcomers had not taught in the elementary and high schools nor were they particularly interested in public school teaching. They were interested primarily in their specialties, in history, physics, literature, or mathematics. They accepted positions in the teachers colleges because collegiate teaching positions were not plentiful and the teachers colleges, though their salaries were not spectacular, frequently offered more than that paid to the lowest ranks at the universities. Even today many a teachers college can, and must, offer the new doctor of philosophy four thousand dollars a year or more with an assistant professorship when the best the same candidate is offered at the largest universities is an instructorship at perhaps thirty-six hundred dollars.

These new recruits from the graduate schools brought to the teachers colleges a new level of scholarship. They brought also many of the prejudices of their university professors regarding educators and education. In the university it had been the custom to speak scornfully of education and to think of education as something with which the college professor has nothing to do. But in the teachers college such scorn was a different matter, for here the educator was not to be so easily pushed around. The president of the college and the dean were educators and proud of it. The newly arrived doctor of philosophy in physics or history found that his scorn of things educational made him *persona non grata*. Often he became embittered and in his bitterness increased his scorn for professional educators, but he learned to be careful where he made his remarks.

Well-concealed scorn is not a stable basis for a harmonious working relationship, however, and the battle between the subject-matter specialists and the educators continues unabated in many a teachers college.

# CHAPTER VII

# THE AMERICAN TEACHER

In a typical suburban community of 10,000 population located in almost any part of these United States there are between 2,000 and 2,500 children enrolled in the public school. Of the adults in this community between seventy-five and one hundred are teachers, principals, or supervisors in the public schools. In the same population there are only twelve or fifteen judges and lawyers and about the same number of physicians. There are about ten clergymen and six dentists. In terms of numbers the teachers are clearly the leading professional group.

In terms of influence, also, the teachers seem to stand far ahead of the others. The typical citizen goes through life without ever meeting a judge, in his official capacity, face to face; and at only a few times during his life does he consult a lawyer. If he follows the advice given in the dentifrice advertisements he sees his dentist twice a year, and he probably consults a physician no more often. Perhaps half these citizens find themselves under the direct influence of their ministers, priests, or rabbis for an average of an hour or two each week, exclusive of the fishing season; the other half meets with members of the clergy only on the occasions of weddings and funerals.

But almost all of these citizens for approximately one-fifth of their lives spend five days a week for thirty-six or forty weeks each year under the direct influence of a teacher or teachers. That the influence of the teaching profession is enormous, for good or for ill, can scarcely be doubted.

These teachers, if we are to include all those in our nation, range in age from eighteen to well over seventy and in educational background from less than a complete high-school education to doctoral degrees. In intelligence the brightest are of genius or near-genius level and at the other extreme are some whose perspicacity is considerably below that of the average pupil in their classes.

Despite the tremendous range we can make some generalizations about teachers. They are younger than any other professional group; three-fourths of them are women; nearly all consider themselves underpaid and most of them are.

Despite the influx of new and young teachers the average age of teachers is rising due to the greater proportion of individuals who are now making a lifetime career of teaching. In 1890 only about 8 per cent of all teachers were over forty-five. By 1940 the figure had risen to about 20 per cent. But even today the average teacher is undoubtedly younger than the average member of any other major profession, probably well under thirty-five if we include those in cities and villages of all sizes.

The youthfulness of teachers in the past resulted from the common practice of bright young men and women using teaching as a steppingstone. After a few years the men would move on to business or to another profession and many of the women would marry. But this custom is becoming far less prevalent. In most of our states a teaching certificate now takes far too long to acquire for it to be used as a temporary step in a career. And under the pressure of the teacher shortage many communities have lifted their ban on married-women teachers, so that now a great many of these women combine marriage with a teaching career.

The ratio of the sexes in teaching has fluctuated with the years. In 1880 two teachers out of every five were men. The proportion of men declined steadily until 1930 when only one out of every six was a man. Since 1930 the proportion of men in the profession has increased slowly. At the beginning of World War II one out of five was a man. The figure decreased during the war, but since 1946 it has risen rapidly. While we have no reliable and completely up-to-date figures it seems likely that the proportion of men in 1953 is about one in four. This proportion is certain to go higher because more than half of the recent graduates of teachers colleges have been men.

The recent increase in the proportion of men teachers is the result of two things. One is increased salaries. When these increases are measured against the increased cost of living in recent years the rise in salaries is slight, but even a slight increase has encouraged men to enter the profession. The other factor is one which I cannot document but which grows out of an impression gained from talking with hundreds of prospective teachers. This is the increased emphasis which young people of today place upon security and the relatively lessened emphasis they place upon excitement and adventure. I am not at all sure that this is a good sign, even though it has brought us more men teachers. But at least it is understandable.

The late 1920s, if my memory does not mislead me, was an age of great expectations. Each of us in college then fully expected to do something extraordinary with his life. He expected to run for the Senate, to make a killing on the stock market, or to build up a great and prosperous business. But first of all he planned to spend a little time adventuring around the world à la Richard Halliburton. And in his spare time he planned to write a novel which would retire Hemingway to the minor leagues. The teaching profession, which offered low salaries, little prestige, little chance for advancement, and no visible adventure, did not interest us. Even though I attended a teachers college I cannot recall a single man of my acquaintance who really expected to make a lifetime career of teaching.

Of course most of us were sidetracked from our adventurous plans. The depression put an end to dreams of sudden wealth via the stock market, and though many of us eventually saw the "atolls in the sun" it was as men in uniform rather than as freewheeling individual adventurers. But it is characteristic that the men of my generation are still planning to write the Great American Novel one of these days.

The college men with whom I talk today have no such fanciful delusions. They have a very different fantasy: they want security above all else. Perhaps this results from the depression and the war. The young men of today were very small boys at the time of the great depression, but it has left its mark upon them. The war too has left its mark, even upon those who had little direct part in it. The men who spent months in foxholes came to think of nothing as so desirable as a nice safe job back home, a job which would require no travel, would involve no risk, and which would make possible a stable home life. These men could not possibly understand the Richard Halliburtons of the twenties and perhaps it is just as well. Nor could they understand the reckless hedonism of a Millay.

Even the younger men, those who have never seen a foxhole and who have yet to view the far places of the earth from the decks of a crowded transport, are driven by their unhappy anticipations to prefer security to adventure. They believe that teaching with its relatively stable employment, its freedom from physical hazards, and its pension systems offers such security. That this belief is bringing more men into the teaching profession is most fortunate. It is to be hoped, however, that the desire for security is not their only motive.

II

Teachers are recruited from all levels of our socioeconomic structure but the number of teachers is not at all proportionate to the number of people at each level. In *Teachers for Our Times*, published in 1944 as a report of the Commission of Teacher Education of the American Council on Education, it was reported that "common observation, supported by such studies as are available, suggests that our teachers predominately come from families relatively modest in circumstances. The sons and daughters of the well to do are apt to enter other occupations; those of the poorest parents often are prevented, by reason of cost, from completing the education required for teaching. The cultural backgrounds of teachers naturally vary, the average level being higher in some sections of the country than in others. On the whole, however, those responsible for their education cannot assume that they have had ready access to great works of art or music or that they have been saturated in literature of the highest quality. They are likely to come of hardworking, substantial stock, and to share the strengths and weakneses of the great bulk of our people."

Coming as they do predominately from the lower middle class our teachers naturally carry with them and tend to pass on to the children the mores, folkways, and customs of that class.

How do the academic abilities of teachers-college students compare with those of students attending other types of colleges? We do not need to guess because the facts are readily available.

The American Council on Education's Psychological Examination for College Freshmen is given annually to entering students at 229 colleges and universities located in all parts of the United States. Included are many types of collegiate institutions. Some are famous, but relatively small, schools, such as Dartmouth College and Clark University. Some are larger schools such as Brooklyn College and the University of Pittsburgh. Among the many less well known colleges are included twenty-two teachers colleges.

The range of abilities found in these various colleges is enormous, passing from an average score of 132 for students of the best college down to an average of only 33 for the worst. (These are raw scores or number of items answered correctly and should not be confused with I.Q.'s.)

Of these 229 institutions none of the teachers colleges ranks among the highest ten on this test, but neither does any teachers college rank among the lowest ten. The average teachers-college score is 2 or 3 per cent lower than the average for all types of colleges, not enough to justify any generalization except to say that on the average teachers college students are not much different in ability from students in other colleges.

There *is* evidence that the students who *enter* teachers colleges are less able than those who enter the more selective professional schools such as those of engineering and law. In the draft-deferment examinations recently given to several thousand college men, the engineering students scored highest and the prospective teachers lowest among the men in professional courses. This is both tragic and understandable. Since a great many of these men had but recently entered their professional schools the differences cannot be attributed to the strengths or the weakness of the schools in which they were currently enrolled. It can be attributed rather to the difference in entrance standards of the various schools. Most professional schools set high entrance standards which exclude all but superior students. They are able to do this because the number of young men wishing to become engineers, lawyers, and physicians is much larger than the number of men needed in these professions. Teachers colleges, too, would like to raise their entrance standards, but in many states, as in my own, they are required by state law to accept all high-school graduates regardless of other evidences of ability or lack of it. It will be difficult to get these entrance requirements changed as long as the shortage of teachers continues; so that the long range solution lies in making teaching a more attractive and more remunerative profession.

But though many teachers colleges must accept the students who are weak academically, they are not required to graduate them; and in many teachers colleges the graduating class is only 30 to 50 per cent as large as the class of entering freshmen. The result of this selection within the college is that *graduating* teachers are not nearly so far below the level of the graduates of other professional courses as might be expected from the scores on the draft-deferment tests. But the work of the teachers colleges would be made much easier—and their prestige would go up—if they were allowed to establish some more reasonable entrance standards.

The facts are bad enough. Those who plan to become teachers ought, it seems, to be definitely superior to other college students, and they are not. But these figures clearly do not justify any feeling of superiority on the part of the liberal arts colleges.

There is one particularly hopeful sign. In the teachers college with which I am most familiar there are sixty freshmen who, on this test, made higher scores than the average made in the highest ranking liberal arts college among those given the test and the majority of these superior students plan to become teachers.

Evidence that teachers as a group possess better general ability than did those of a generation ago is to be found in the test scores of men inducted into the Army during World War I and World War II. In World War I the Army Alpha scores of public school teachers were distinctly lower than those of members of the other learned professions. But a generation later the scores on the Army General Classification Test showed that teachers were no longer an inferior group in terms of the abilities measured by this test. On one sample of men inducted into the Army in 1942, the average scores for a few sample professions were: accountants, 128; medical students, 126; teachers, 124; lawyers, 124. (Medical students rather than graduate physicians were included because this test was given only to enlisted men and all physicians were officers.) The differences among these four groups are not large enough to be important, but the difference between these professional groups and the average of 100 for all vocations is important. (Naomi Stewart, "AGCT Scores of Army Personnel Grouped by Occupations," *Occupations,* Vol. 26, pp. 5–41, 1947.)

### III

But though the average intelligence and the average academic ability of teachers do not appear to be too bad the intelligence and the scholarly abilities of the poorest teacher are very bad indeed.

Most educators are understandably reluctant to publish evidence of the incompetence of even a few of the graduates of their colleges but one such report was published by William S.

Learned and Ben D. Wood (*The Student and His Knowledge,* Carnegie Foundation for the Advancement of Teaching, Bulletin 29, 1938, pp. 38–39).

A highly varied test of many kinds of knowledge was given first to a group of high-school seniors and then to college seniors who were about to become teachers. The lowest 7 per cent of these prospective teachers actually made lower scores than did the upper 36 per cent of the high-school students. And on a one-hundred-word vocabulary test the lowest 30 per cent of the teacher group knew the meaning of fewer than fifty of the words while 29 per cent of the high-school group knew fifty words or more. Yet these college seniors were destined in a few months to be teaching students such as the high-school seniors who excelled them on these tests. If we assume that a minimum requirement for teaching ought to be that the teacher know more than the student, it seems reasonable to ask just who ought to be paid for teaching whom. Some of my more progressive friends have an answer. They say that subject matter isn't really important anyway.

But if you are a typical parent you will surely ask why the college allows such students to graduate and to receive teaching certificates. My answer is not a very good one but at least it has the merit of being truthful.

If all these incompetents were ruthlessly weeded out, the enrollment of the college would suddenly be reduced by at least 10 per cent and possibly by as much as 25 per cent. Moreover the shortage of new teachers, already acute, would be increased by the same percentage. No administration of a state teachers college could possibly face such a drop in enrollment. I do not know whether the legislatures actually apportion funds to the state colleges on the basis of their enrollments but many college and university presidents are convinced that they do. If the happy day ever arrives when legislatures apportion funds to state colleges on the basis of quality of education offered rather than on the basis of number of students enrolled, perhaps something can be done about standards in state colleges.

The solution to this problem will be much easier too when there are enough teachers for all the schools, but this day appears to be a long way off. According to a recent report of the National Commission on Teacher Education and Professional Standards there is immediate need for at least 160,000 new elementary-school teachers. It is estimated that fewer than 33,000 new teachers will be qualified this year. So long as this shortage exists, any weeding out of borderline candidates for the profession can only result in a still greater shortage of teachers.

It is most unfortunate that the entire profession is sometimes ridiculed and discredited because of the stupidities and incompetencies of a few. I want to make it clear that I am talking about the lowest 10 or 20 per cent and not about the typical teacher. For I am convinced that the typical teacher compares favorably in scholarship, intelligence, and common sense with the typical member of any other profession.

But both the profession and the parents must protect themselves and must protect the children against the incompetents at the lower end of the teaching profession. If we are to do this we must be aware of the existence of these incompetents. Educators have sometimes been guilty of overlooking or concealing the facts, but such facts cannot be successfully concealed from the public. The outstandingly able teacher may not be conspicuous in a social group, but the teacher who says "He don't," however important or unimportant that little error in English may be, is extremely conspicuous. Teachers had better remember that when they protest that they are underpaid the school-board member is likely to recall that one conspicuous teacher and to overlook the ones of exceptional ability, particularly if the salary schedule provides equal rewards to all teachers of similar education and experience.

### IV

There has always been a shortage of good teachers, but today there is a shortage of every kind of teacher. In a country in which young people are free to make their own choices as to vocations, it is obvious that such a shortage reflects a reluctance on the part of young men and women to enter the profession. What is the reason for this reluctance?

Many reasons have been given. Low salaries, low prestige, and restrictions on the teacher's social behavior are among those most often mentioned. But one important reason is frequently overlooked. Students most often make their vocational choices at some time between the junior year in high school and the junior year of college. And to girls and even more to boys in the age range from sixteen to twenty teaching has little appeal.

There are several reasons for this. One is that these older adolescents have for ten, twelve, or fourteen years been in close contact with teachers good and bad. They know a great deal about teachers and have seen all the dreariest aspects of their work. If for the same period of time they had been in equally close touch with the work of any other profession, it seems likely that they might be equally reluctant to enter that profession, but they have been spared such proximity. If the boy of eighteen had spent the past twelve years of his life in a law office watching the lawyer in his tiresome work of drawing up wills and contracts, of searching through law books for background information, of trying to collect fees from impecunious malefactors, it is doubtful that he would have any urge to become a lawyer. But his only acquaintance with the field of law comes from occasionally observing a lawyer pleading a sensational murder case, or more likely from hearing highly romanticized accounts of such cases. So he thinks of law as adventurous and exciting.

He cannot possibly think of teaching as exciting because he knows too much about it, and what he knows is not alluring to his adolescent mentality. Should he have been so fortunate as to come under the influence of a really outstanding teacher, this influence might be enough to change his mind. But such teachers have always been rare. If vocational choices were made at the age of thirty-five or forty, or even at the age of twenty-five as was true in the case of many returning veterans, the situation might be much different. By this time he might have become somewhat disillusioned about some of the other professions. His desire to fly off into the bright blue yonder might have subsided somewhat; he might have discovered that there is much monotony in nearly every kind of work.

The fact is that few kinds of work involve so little monotony as does teaching. A good teacher may not repeat his activities more than once each year. A physician, even though he finds no two cases quite identical, may well discover that one set of diseased tonsils looks very much like another, and if he is a specialist he peers down many similar throats every day. To assume that guiding students through history or literature is more monotonous than extracting teeth or tonsils seems farfetched. But it is difficult indeed to make this clear to the student who thinks of the medical profession only in terms of spectacular surgery which is written up in the popular magazines or who gets his ideas from the *Men in White* type of motion picture.

When a male college student chooses his vocation, he spends

a considerable amount of time imagining himself in the role into which the chosen vocation will thrust him. At the age of eighteen or twenty he is still trying to establish himself as a normal adult, free of parental control and of all other controls which may interfere with his adult role. He can comfortably think of himself as an engineer, a reporter, a lawyer, or even a salesman because it seems to him that men in all of these vocations are accepted as normal male adults subject only to such social restrictions as apply to all who live within the laws. But when he thinks of himself as a teacher he becomes uncomfortable because he observes that the teacher is subject to many of the restrictions from which he as a maturing adolescent is struggling to free himself. In many communities the teacher must never be seen in a cocktail lounge, and there are still some in which teachers may not smoke. In smaller communities he may be practically required to teach a Sunday-school class or lead a boy-scout troop. In many cases he is quite willing to take part in such community activities, but he doesn't like to think that he *must* do so as a part of his job. He wants to be as free to decide in each case for himself as are members of other vocations. He probably has no great desire to frequent bars, but he wants to be free to decide about such things for himself. What he most wants at this age is the normal adult freedoms, and so he rejects a teaching career in favor of almost any other vocation.

The girl of the same age feels much the same way. If she becomes a nurse, a stenographer, a salesgirl, or an airline hostess, she can live just about as she pleases in her free time, or that is the impression she gets from observing young women in such jobs. But she fears that if she becomes a teacher she will immediately find herself in a very different role, one in which all the busybodies in the community will feel free to tell her when she must get in nights, whom she may not date, and what she may not drink. Even if she has never tasted any liquid stronger than a lemon coke, she dislikes the idea of having all the Aunt Nellies of the neighborhood pass judgment upon her choice of drinks. So she decides to become a nurse or a stenographer even though the salary may be even less than in teaching.

Though the teacher has, in recent years, gained more freedom to live a normal life and to make normal adult decisions than was true a generation ago, teachers still do not find themselves fully accepted as normal adults in the community. They are expected to be paragons of virtue, and the simple fact is that very few normal men or women in their twenties want to be thought of as paragons of anything quite so dull. They may not, as individuals, desire to kick over the traces a great deal, but they would like to have people think they have the same freedom to do so as have other adults. They know that if they become teachers everyone will assume that they have no such freedom. So they do not choose to be teachers.

While it seems necessary to offer this explanation for the reluctance of young people to enter the profession, it is to be hoped that what has been said will not dissuade able young men and women from becoming teachers. Many of us who have tried other vocations and have then returned to teaching have discovered that as teachers we have not lost any important freedoms. We can testify that, even with conditions as they are now, teaching can be a very satisfying and rewarding way of life. We do not feel in the least downtrodden or frustrated, and not all of us waste our time feeling sorry for ourselves. We do not find our work at all monotonous or dull. We most certainly do not envy those who devote their lives to selling real estate or cigarettes, or to drawing up wills or deeds. We are not at all jealous of those who make a living extracting teeth, designing factories, or building roads. We know that these jobs must be done but we do not wish to do them. We prefer to deal with young people and with great ideas. Neither will ever seem dull.

# CHAPTER VIII

# FACTS OR METHODS?

The high school in a small Middle Western city had a vacancy last fall for a teacher of business law. In the city was a young attorney whose law practice was not yet very remunerative and who decided that he would like to teach for a year or two while getting acquainted with the community, which was new to him.

The young man went to the city superintendent of schools to offer his services. His qualifications included a liberal arts degree with honors from a famous university and a law degree from one of the better law schools. His experience included two years as an instructor in the law school from which he had received his degree.

To his amazement he learned that he was not considered qualified to teach even an elementary course in business law in the public high school. Before teaching in such a school he must have a state certificate, and to qualify for such a certificate he must take a series of courses in education, including a semester of practice teaching. The superintendent explained that he had no choice in the matter, that certification standards were set by the state department of education on the basis of recommendations of the college of education at the state university.

Eventually the position was filled by a young man who had

taken only two courses in business law and who had no legal experience whatever but who had completed the necessary course in educational principles, methods, and practice teaching.

The experience of this attorney was by no means exceptional. It is quite true that the certification laws in practically every state would make it impossible for the public schools to employ a Toscanini as a high-school music teacher or an Einstein as a teacher of algebra. If Socrates were with us he might be employed by a college (if he were willing to take the loyalty oath, which seems unlikely), but he surely could not secure a position in a public high school.

Whether such certification laws represent codified nonsense or a reasonable protection of the child has long been a subject for debate. Those who hold that they represent nonsense maintain that the essential qualification of the teacher is a thorough knowledge of his subject; they contend that the best musician is the best teacher of music and the best mathematician is the best teacher of mathematics.

Those who defend the present laws maintain that teaching is a profession calling for highly developed professional skills which are quite apart from knowledge of the subject taught. They hold that an Einstein may very well be an extremely poor teacher of high-school algebra because of inadequate understanding of the mental processes of adolescents or because of an inability to communicate at the level of high-school students. These skills of communication and this understanding of the student can, they think, be taught, and they are taught in the required courses in education.

But there is a third possibility. It may be that teaching does require something more than knowledge of subject matter but that this something more is not always successfully instilled

through courses in education and practice teaching and is sometimes possessed or developed by those who have never been
exposed to such courses.

Our young lawyer would, I think, have been an excellent
teacher, and it was unfortunate that the rules were not sufficiently flexible to permit his employment. With his intelligence,
curiosity, and energy he would have quickly discovered satisfactory methods of presenting his material and of dealing with
students in a learning situation. The man who did get the job
was probably too limited in his knowledge of law to teach the
subject well, despite his greater background of courses in
education. It does not automatically follow that the study of
educational methods is useless or unimportant, but it does seem
reasonable to assume that methods do not take the place of a
thorough knowledge of the subject taught any more than
knowledge of subject takes the place of teaching skills.

The teacher whose knowledge does not go beyond the subject matter which he is to teach will certainly be a poor teacher.
If he keeps just one page ahead of the student he will be unable
to examine ideas critically or to explore relationships. He will
be uncertain, timid, and afraid of student questions and criticism. This was the source of much of the poor instruction in
the Army. When the instructor was teaching something he
himself had learned only yesterday, he quickly learned to
silence all questions lest his own limitations be discovered. But
when the Army officer possessed an exhaustive knowledge of
his subject he often became an excellent teacher. (In recent
years the military academies have placed increased emphasis on
methods of teaching. I once heard a major general observe that
the academy at West Point is, and ought to be, essentially a
teachers college. He pointed out that the typical officer spends

perhaps three or four years of his life leading men in combat and thirty years or more training and preparing men for combat. Training is a form of teaching and the officer, whether he likes it or not, devotes most of his years to teaching.)

A few progressive educators have implied that knowledge of subject matter is not necessary for the teacher, since the school should not concern itself with subject matter but only with the "growth" of the child. A teaching method has developed in which the teacher takes great care not to give out any information but acts only as a friendly guide. The students sit down and discuss a problem, sharing their information in an effort to find their own answers.

In dealing with some problems, such as deciding on the decorations for the dance Saturday night, this technique works very well. In others, such as trying to discover the meaning of a poem, the sharing of ideas may work reasonably well, though it would be well if the teacher had a few ideas too. But some teachers have tried to use this method in discovering facts of a highly technical sort, and in such cases the method becomes ridiculous. One of my colleagues has a name for this sort of thing; he calls it "the sharing of ignorance method."

Unless the teacher is to be limited to some such method he will need to know his subject thoroughly. But we still are faced with the problem of determining how much the teacher needs to know about methods of teaching.

II

Teachers can be and have been selected on the basis of knowledge of subject matter, on the basis of knowledge of teaching methods, or upon some combination of the two. The unhappy fact is that whichever method is used we get some good teachers and some very poor teachers.

Those schools—in most cases they are colleges or universities —which select teachers on the basis of competency in a field of knowledge without regard to teaching skills frequently maintain individuals on their staffs who are downright incompetent in terms of communicating ideas to their students. But those schools which select teachers on the basis of knowledge of methodology also support many incompetent teachers.

Good teaching is easily recognized by the student but is difficult for anyone to diagnose. It appears that such teaching involves a third factor—something above and beyond both knowledge of subject and knowledge of method. To say that this third factor is the personality of the teacher is probably correct, although too vague to be of much help. In its finest development teaching is an artistic skill of the very highest order. There are probably as many first-rate teachers in the land as there are first-rate poets, concert pianists, or painters. But while the nation can get along pretty well with a few dozen of each of these other artists, it must have over a million teachers. It should come as no surprise that most teachers teach with about as much distinction as the girl next door plays the piano, assuming that the girl next door has had many years of musical training and usually strikes the right keys but lacks the essential something which makes a great pianist. I do not at all mean to imply that teachers are born rather than made as a product of their experiences. But it does appear likely that some of the essential ingredients are personality traits which are generally determined before the prospective teacher reaches maturity, and that other ingredients are the direct results of his intelligence level or even of his energy output.

The good teacher must possess a lively intellectual curiosity and a sufficient amount of energy and critical ability to assure that he will find it more satisfying to keep out of ruts than to get into them. Lacking these things he is certain to become a pedant, for a pedant is merely one who lacks the curiosity to explore new ideas, the energy to develop them, or the intelligence to examine them critically. The candidate for the teaching profession should be sufficiently grown up to be reasonably free of prejudices, resentments, and defensiveness. He will like children and enjoy working with them but will not be gushy or sentimental in his attitude toward them. Given these characteristics and a thorough knowledge of the subject matter with which he is to deal, he is ready to learn something about the more technical aspects of teaching.

In the modern teachers college the courses called "education" are by no means limited to courses in method. In some of these schools methods courses have all but disappeared. But somewhere along the line the teacher must become aware that teaching and learning are very complicated processes which involve much more than recitation of facts. This is not a new discovery and is improperly attributed to the progressives; Socrates understood it very well a long time ago.

Teachers who have to drill on facts because their pupils are required to pass factual tests find confusion and difficulty in reconciling this with theories of education taught in teachers colleges. But an understanding of the psychology of learning will help the teacher to know what methods are most appropriate and effective in any given learning situation. Some learning involves complicated thought processes or problem solving. Some is essentially a matter of perception. Some consists of the development of new habits or the elimination of old ones, and some of these habits can be learned by drill.

Many critics of the modern schools have thought that we should make more use of drill, and in some few cases they may be right; but surely the importance of drill can easily be over-emphasized. Even the teaching of a fact is rarely a simple matter of drill.

Columbus discovered America in 1492. This is usually considered to be a fact. But it is also a statement of a complicated relationship, a relationship involving a man whom we call Columbus (but whom the Spaniards called Colón), a place we call America (he did not call it that and never knew that he had found a new world), and a point in time marked 1492 on our calendar. Of course Columbus was not the only man on his ship, and there were three ships in all; hence, a good many men might be said to have discovered America at the same time. On second thought all that was discovered in 1492 was a group of Atlantic islands which happened to be near the shores of the New World.

Nor was Columbus's little band of mariners the first to reach the New World. The red men had long been here, and it seems somewhat presumptuous for us to assume that the arrival of white men is discovery and that the arrival of men of other pigmentation is not discovery. Columbus was not even the first white captain to arrive. Long before his time there had been the Vikings and possibly others as well.

Learning the historical fact of the discovery of the New World is actually the learning of a very complicated set of relationships. The child who learns to recite "Columbus discovered America in 1492" has only begun to learn. The really important learning lies ahead of him and it cannot be accomplished by drill.

Two plus two equals four. This fact is also a relationship involving the numbers "2" and "4" and the words "plus" and "equals." The child reading or hearing this statement of fact may be able to learn the meaning of "4" but only if he already knows the meaning of "2," of "plus," and of "equals." Otherwise the statement is to him just so much gobbledy-gook.

Equally confusing to the small child is the statement about the discovery of America. This statement will convey its intended meaning to the school child in Ohio only if he knows that Columbus was a man long before the state capitol was named for him, if he knows clearly what is meant by the word "discovered" (do *you* know?), and if the date 1492 has some meaning for him.

If this seems too simple, let us try it at our own level of difficulty. I pick up a textbook in philosophy and read that "to Leibnitz, the monads are God's perpetual fulguration." This is a very enlightening fact—or is it? Whether or not it enlightens depends upon my previous knowledge. If I think Leibnitz is a city in Germany, confuse monads with gonads, and am hazy about the meaning of fulguration, the memorization of this fact leaves me little better off than if I had spent my time reading the funny papers.

I am not trying to discredit the teaching of facts; there has been too much of that already. But I am trying to make it clear that the lines between facts, relationships, and ideas are fuzzy ones and that effective learning of any of these involves much more than learning to say a group of words in some formal sequence, *i.e.*, effective learning involves much more than drill. I hope to make it equally clear that the learning of all facts is dependent upon the prior knowledge of the learner. It follows that the teaching of even the simplest facts requires, on the part of the teacher, a great deal of knowledge about the learners and about the nature of learning, as well as a knowledge of the facts to be learned. If the teacher erroneously assumes that her second-grade pupils understand what is meant by the word "plus," all her efforts to teach them to add will be in vain.

It seems likely that really competent teachers have always understood this, or at any rate that they have become aware of it after some years of teaching experience. But the beginning teacher often does not understand it unless it has been pointed out to him and illustrated. The assumption, frequently made, that anyone who knows the facts will be a competent teacher shows the most abysmal ignorance of the nature of the learning process. Socrates was a great teacher, not because he knew the facts alone, but because he knew how to draw out the students in such a way that *they* came to understand the facts, the principles, or the relationships. He was a master of one technique of teaching.

It is quite true that Socrates never took a course in education nor even one in psychology, but to conclude from this that no teacher can profit from such a course is to commit a logical fallacy of which Socrates himself would never have been guilty.

Socrates knew a great deal about the psychology of learning. Let us not assume that every beginning teacher has a similar knowledge nor that he is incapable of gaining at least a little of it.

### III

Learning to read is probably the most difficult of all the steps in formal education, but most of us learned so long ago and read so easily now that we have all but forgotten the difficulty. Difficulty of learning is entirely a relative matter. The difficulty is relative to the learner's inherent intelligence, to his past experience with related things, ideas, and symbols, and to the complexity of the new idea which he is trying to grasp.

It is not very difficult for you or for me to learn to read a few words of a new language such as Portuguese. It is reasonably easy because the component parts of the new learning are already familiar to us. We already possess the concepts expressed by the words. We know the letters of which they are made. We have at least a vague idea of how some of the combinations of letters may be pronounced, though in this we may well be mistaken. Most important of all we know that in reading a Western language one starts at the upper left-hand corner of the page, proceeds to the right, and then drops down to the left-hand side of the line below. We know the meaning of capitals and of most of the punctuation marks, and if the writer himself was literate these marks are so placed as to make our reading easier.

But to the nonreader, however intelligent he may be, none of these things is obvious. He may, like the boy in Kipling's story, wonder whether one reads the black or the white part of the page. We become better aware of tl.e difficulty when we try to read a language totally different from our own, a language such as Chinese, though even here we have the advantage of much prior related learning.

Probably you cannot remember much about your difficulties in learning to read, but perhaps you do recall your difficulties with the much simpler, but somewhat similar, problem of learning to identify the stars and the constellations. A friend takes you out on a moonless night intent upon teaching you to recognize his old friends in the heavens.

"That," he says, "is Polaris." You look up along his arm and see dozens of stars, all very much alike. You do not doubt his wisdom but you have little idea which of the dots it is which so excites him.

"See," he says jubilantly, "you can locate it by the fact that it lies on a line extended from Ursa Major."

"Oh!" you say, "Ursa Major." But you still see only a myriad of stars. You see no Ursa Major and even if you remember a few words of Latin you can recognize nothing even vaguely resembling a bear, either great or small.

"And that," he says, turning around and again pointing, "is Sirius. See, it lies on a line extended from the belt of Orion. Sirius is the brightest of all stars and so is easy to identify."

You look obediently but you see no hunter and certainly not the belt of a hunter; just a lot of scrambled little dots of light with no pattern whatever. Finally you do notice that one seems much brighter than the others. Now it is your turn to point.

"Oh, yes," you say, "I see it now—that big one with the reddish tint."

"That," says your astronomer friend with a patient air, "that is not a star. That is Jupiter."

"Oh!" you say feebly. "Looks like a star, doesn't it?" At this point you become aware of a stiff neck and suggest to your friend that you would like to go back in the house for a fast game of fan-tan. Fortunately you are not graded on this lesson, and no report of progress is made to your parents.

The position of the child learning to read is less fortunate and much more difficult. The words on the page before him are as meaningless and as unpatterned as the constellations. But while there are only a few dozen constellations there are thousands of words to be learned. Some nouns like "cat" and "dog" represent visible things which are familiar to the child. A few adjectives like "big" and "pretty" have already become useful in his spoken language. But there are many others, such as "except," "minus," and "alike," whose precise meaning is not really clear to the small child. There are still others which sound alike but which do not look alike and which have different meanings, "to," "too," and "two," for example.

All this is obvious to us but is very confusing to the child learning to read. His confusion must be understood by the teacher. Moreover, the teacher must understand what steps to take to clear up the confusion.

Effective reading is not a matter of looking at each letter, putting the letters together into words, and then organizing the words into sentences. If you are an average adult reader you will read this page in less than two minutes. If you are an exceptionally fast reader you may read it in less than thirty seconds. In that amount of time you cannot possibly look at each individual letter or even at each individual word. But you can grasp all the ideas contained on the page, and you will grasp the ideas more clearly if you do not try to proofread, examining each vowel and consonant. There is adequate evidence that fast readers, on the average, comprehend what they read better than do slow readers even though this is contrary to popular opinion. Knowing this, the competent teacher of reading lets the children start by recognizing words or phrases. The child will need to learn the alphabet, but this learning does not necessarily precede reading.

The teacher of reading must himself be able to read, but such ability alone does not give assurance of the ability to teach others to read effectively.

## IV

I think there is little room for doubt that much that is taught in education courses is of real use to the prospective teacher, though I may be suspected of prejudice, since a part of my work includes the teaching of such courses.

But why have courses in education been so vigorously attacked by the intellectual critics of modern education? The answer is a complicated one, but part of it, I think, lies in the fact that we have expanded our course offerings beyond all reason. Particularly in the large universities where it is thought necessary to have a catalogue of courses which rivals the phone book in size, simple ideas which could be developed in a few hours have been expanded into full five-credit courses a semester in length. The overlapping among such courses is so great that a student may sit for hours without hearing anything really new. In the effort to make much out of little and to take up the time, ideas have been, as one graduate student put it, "vagued up." A special language has been developed which is meaningless to the uninitiated and which has no very clear meaning to anyone.

To solve this dilemma by eliminating all courses in education would be to throw out the baby with the bath water. A better solution would be to simplify course offerings as much as possible, decide what is really important, eliminate the nonessential, make a real effort to avoid duplication, and rewrite the education textbooks in clear and simple English.

Some effort is being made in this direction, particularly in the smaller teachers colleges whose faculties are not overweighted with specialists as are the universities. But much remains to be done.

# CHAPTER IX

# WHATEVER BECAME OF THE THREE R's?

Any gathering of citizens discussing the problems of public education can agree on at least one thing: The schools should give more attention to the fundamentals. They are, after all, fundamental.

But if anyone is so impertinent as to ask just what is meant by "the fundamentals," the group is likely to become less harmonious. On the importance of the three R's there is usually agreement, at least so far as the elementary school is concerned; but what about character training? Most of the discussants will agree that such training is fundamental, but some hold that it falls within the province of the home and the church, and there is no agreement at all as to just how character is taught.

Is music fundamental or a frill? On this there is little agreement, for in each community there is at least a minority of parents who think that music is important even in elementary education. How about history, health education, and the teaching of democratic principles?

It is at the secondary level that the problem is the most difficult. If the three R's are the only fundamentals, how is the high school to occupy its time? Are we to drag out the teaching of reading, writing, and arithmetic through twelve years of schooling? If not, are algebra and geometry as fundamental at the high-school level as is arithmetic in the lower grades? Is the study of Shakespeare's tragedies, which might be considered an advanced form of reading, as fundamental to the seventeen-year-old as is elementary reading to the younger child?

To some it seems that homemaking, as taught in such courses as child care, food preparation, and clothing making, is fundamental for most girls. Of course these things *can* be learned at home, or at any rate they could be in grandmother's day. Are the mothers of today teaching them, or do they want the schools to do it?

While some parents are asking the schools to eliminate the fads and frills, other parents organize themselves into very powerful pressure groups which insist that the high school maintain a winning football team and a marching band complete with shapely drum majorettes. It is rarely the teachers who demand these things. Many a city superintendent or a high-school principal would like to deemphasize athletics if the board of education would help him in facing the inevitable criticism.

A marching band is pleasant to the eye and to the ear, but the uniforms and instruments are expensive and the necessary training takes a great deal of the student's time. These things give the youth some training in discipline, but they can hardly be described as really essential to education. Yet the critical parent should remember that the demand for such things comes from the public much more often than from the teachers as a group.

Of course the teacher whose specific job it is to coach the football team or to direct the marching band will naturally defend the activities which have become so closely identified with his livelihood. There is a vicious circle here—or anyway a circle. It comes about like this.

In the community there is a small but influential group of citizens which feels that some activity of special interest to them should be added to the high-school curriculum. Perhaps these are the fly-fishermen of the community. They become convinced that if all boys could become interested in the battle of wits with a fighting rainbow there would be a great reduction of juvenile delinquency. These young fishermen would be profitably occupied in their spare hours. Instead of standing in front of the corner drugstore or bending over a pool table in hot pursuit of the eight ball, they would be out in God's great out-of-doors getting close to nature and learning real he-man sportsmanship.

Our adult fishermen now approach the superintendent of schools at the weekly Kiwanis luncheon and make their proposal. The superintendent is doubtful. He explains that the curriculum is already full, that there is no spare time, that the equipment would cost money, and that there is no one to teach the new sport. But all his objections are answered. This new activity can be carried on during week ends so as not to interfere with other school activities; the Izaak Walton League will provide some discarded equipment—enough for a start; and some of the members will be glad to show the boys how to fly-cast. They will even provide the transportation out to Mud Lake.

The superintendent is still a little dubious. But after all, these are influential citizens and delinquency really is a serious problem. Besides, the chairman of the board of education is an ardent fly-fisherman.

The superintendent agrees to pass the suggestion on to the high-school principal. The principal too has his doubts. But all he is asked to do is to get the boys together, tell them of the plan, and make arrangements for them to meet the fly casters at the appropriate time. He can hardly refuse to do this much.

So the first season passes. Many of the boys have a pretty good time and some of them even learn to fly-cast. There is no perceptible drop in the delinquency rate; in fact a couple of the boys are arrested for fishing out of season, but after all you can't expect too much right away.

When the next season rolls around some of the downtown sportsmen show a noticeable lack of interest in giving up their Saturdays to offering free lessons in fly casting when they would prefer to do some fishing themselves. They did their part in getting the project started. Let someone else carry it on. Besides some of their fishermen friends are complaining that the high-school boys are getting most of the fish and scaring away those they don't catch.

The high-school principal, now under pressure from the boys, goes to the Kiwanis Club and the Izaak Walton League to plead for more castoff equipment and for some men to give their time to the fishing project. The Kiwanians are somewhat sympathetic but explain that they have no more castoff equipment and that they find themselves pretty busy on Saturdays. They make some helpful suggestions. Why not have some of the teachers, who don't work Saturdays anyway, take over the instruction? As for equipment, why doesn't the school buy some? They buy football uniforms and band instruments; why shouldn't they spend a little on fly rods and reels?

So it comes to pass that several high-school teachers find themselves drafted to be supervisors of fishermen on Saturdays. And the superintendent of schools finds on his desk a requisition for three dozen fly rods, split bamboo—9 feet. He hits the ceiling, but when he comes down and talks to the principal he finds himself signing the requisition while sadly shaking his head and wondering where the money is coming from.

Comes another spring, and the teachers who have had the experience of teaching fishing on Saturdays wait upon the principal as a delegation. They protest that it is unfair to require them to give up their week ends when other teachers are free, and besides some of the boys work on Saturday and so are denied the advantages of fly casting. Fishing, these teachers are convinced, should be integrated into the week's work, just as are music and athletic activities. It wouldn't hurt even to give the boys an occasional afternoon off to participate in the new sport, since the pursuit of the elusive trout has proved to be one of the more popular extracurricular activities.

After a good deal of soul searching the principal agrees. One of the teachers, Mr. Troutstream, has become particularly interested in the new sport and suggests that he would be glad to take the responsibility for coordinating the fly-fishing activities. He is given a new office complete with locked cabinets for storing rods, reels, and double tapered lines, and is officially named Coordinator of Fly Casting. It soon develops that Mr. Troutstream's new duties take so much of his time that he cannot continue his old duties as a teacher of algebra, and so a new algebra teacher is added to the staff. The principal is not too unhappy about this because Mr. Troutstream was never much of an algebra teacher anyway. In fact, he was so bad and there had been so many complaints from students that the principal had been wondering how he could get rid of him. But at his new duties Troutstream is a whiz.

At the next meeting of the curriculum committee the new coordinator, who was once a mere teacher of algebra, has a proposal to make. He describes in glowing terms the educational advantages of fly casting. He tells how it develops eye-hand coordination, how it introduces the boy to nature and thus stimulates his interest in biology. He emphasizes its value in teaching sportsmanship and its importance in reducing delinquency, though his statistics on the latter point are a little vague. He suggests that such a valuable activity should receive credit toward graduation. Not much credit, of course; half a credit will do. Just enough to indicate the recognition given by the school to the part played by fly casting in the development of the whole boy. Naturally it will be an elective; but it might be accepted as a substitute for physical education.

The curriculum committee agrees that half a credit would be reasonable, and so fly casting is elevated from the position of an extracurricular activity to that of a cocurricular one.

The years pass. The coordinator of fly-casting activities is now head of the department of applied ichthyology. He is the author of the textbook *Dynamic Fly Casting and Its Implications for Curriculum Construction.* This is not a very literate book. In fact, it had to be completely rewritten by the publisher before it could be published at all. But it is the first in its field and so becomes widely read; its author becomes an authority.

Mr. Troutstream's department now consists of six men and five women teachers, for naturally it has occurred to someone that applied ichthyology is no less valuable for girls than for boys. Most of these younger teachers have been trained in the new sequence of courses now offered by State Teachers College, for when the teachers college heard about the popularity of fly casting in the high school they were quick to seize upon this opportunity to meet the needs of the expanding curriculum. These younger teachers have received credit toward their master's degrees for courses in Fly-tying, Rod-winding, Overhand-casting, Roll-casting, Special Techniques for Use along Brushy Banks, and Landing-net Manipulation. One wrote a master's thesis on "Casting a Dry Fly into a Hard Wind and Its Significance in Character Education."

At the moment everyone in the field is agog about the new spinning technique which threatens to replace the old style of casting altogether. Several of the teachers have attended a workshop which the state university offers for teachers of the new technique.

At both the teachers college and the university there were a few old die-hards who protested the emphasis being given to applied ichthyology, but these reactionaries were easily over-ruled, for it was known that they were subject-matter-minded and that their years of study of such archaic topics as history, philosophy, and literature had left them completely ignorant of the newer trends in education. Fly casting had arrived.

When the local newspaper gave a four-page spread to the high school, three of the pages were devoted to fly casting and related activities. This article, which received favorable attention from educators and the public, was complete with handsome pictures of pretty high-school girls in shorts landing some large salmon which had been provided for the occasion by the local fish market.

At a meeting of the high-school curriculum committee this spring, Mr. Troutstream of the department of applied ichthyology made another proposal. He pointed out that his department had become the most popular in the school. But that even now a few boys and even more girls were failing to avail themselves of its advantages. And these were the very boys and girls who needed these courses most. He could see only one solution. Fly casting and related courses should be required of all students.

There was vigorous debate. Most of the teachers agreed that fly casting was important but could not see how another requirement could be added to the curriculum. But the head of the applied ichthyology department had an answer to that. Something, he agreed, would have to go. He had done a good deal of thinking about it and had talked with a number of people downtown. They had agreed with him that some of the things taught in the school were impractical, that the curriculum should be more closely related to modern life. He had examined the present curriculum and found that while Greek and Latin had long since been eliminated there remained one relic of the dead and forgotten past. This, he said sadly, was algebra. He would be sorry to see it go. Surely no one could accuse him of being prejudiced against mathematics because he had once been an algebra teacher himself. But algebra is not dynamic and does not fit the needs of today's adolescent. It will have to go.

At this point a group of irate citizens start writing letters to the local newspaper demanding that the schools get rid of the fads and frills. Their special target is the department of applied ichthyology with its numerous courses in fly casting and the related arts. They point out that this one frivolous department gets 17 per cent of the school budget; that a special gymnasium has been built for it so that casting skills would not be lost during the winter months; that its teachers are the most highly paid on the entire faculty.

A committee of citizens calls upon the superintendent. The superintendent, now a tired and elderly man, recognizes the leader of the committee as the one-time fisherman who first proposed the Saturday fishing trip and whose arthritis has long since prevented him from wading in icy waters. The superintendent thinks back over his years as a schoolman and wonders why he ever left the farm.

## II

Though the people responsible are prone to defend all of the activities in which children engage in school, it is probably not unfair to say that some schools, perhaps many schools, do encourage a considerable amount of activity which is pleasant but essentially frivolous. Many of these activities have developed in response to demands of isolated groups in the community, groups which make their suggestions without regard to the fundamental purposes of the school.

Much of the difficulty results from our failure to decide which things are fundamental, and for this failure all citizens must accept some part of the responsibility.

It is essential that we make a clear distinction between fundamental objectives and fundamental skills. The three R's are skills rather than objectives. They are not ends but means toward ends.

When people speak of the three R's they presumably mean "reading, 'riting, and 'rithmetic." We cannot be certain even of this, because one organization which has taken for its slogan "Teach the three R's" gives most of its attention to character training and the teaching of patriotism.

No doubt we can all agree on the meaning of reading and arithmetic, but the meaning of writing is less obvious. Does it mean penmanship, or does it refer to the skills involved in expressing ourselves in written language, skills involving grammar, rhetoric, and logic? Probably most people intend the latter definition, though there are surely some who think of writing as skill in the execution of script.

Skill in the fundamental processes of arithmetic surely appears to be essential to all citizens. Without such skill it would be impossible to keep a checking account or compute one's income tax. Of course these require only rather simple arithmetic, and the fact that many people find an income tax computation difficult suggests that some of our older adults, as well as the younger ones, are less than perfect in their arithmetical skills. The more advanced forms of arithmetic, computing the cube root for example, are used so rarely by most of us as to raise legitimate question concerning the value of their being taught. But some knowledge of decimals is surely essential to all of us who are to use American money.

All the arithmetic skills which are necessary to the average housewife or clerk can be taught to the average twelve-year-old if he is adequately motivated and has good instruction. To make simple arithmetic one of the essentials of a high-school curriculum is an unnecessary prolongation of infancy.

As we have said, reading, like the other R's, is not an end in itself. But as a means to an end—as a means to many ends—it is surely of the highest order of importance. The ability to read opens up to the individual possessing such ability the vast written record of the knowledge of the ages and of the present day. In a literate society reading is an essential form of communication. In our own nation today the man who cannot read is a man almost isolated from the society which surrounds him. To the unfeeling he is occasionally an object of humor; to the more sensitive observer he is always an object of pity.

We saw some of these pitiable individuals in the Army. A few were morons, incapable of learning to read, but many were men of good native intelligence who by some misfortune had been denied the opportunity to gain even the rudiments of a formal education. To them the signs posted on the bulletin board were as meaningless as are Chinese street signs to you and me. They found themselves charged with breaking rules of which they had never heard. A letter from home was a mere slip of paper unless some more fortunate friend could be found to act as interpreter. Often the inability to read became so great a source of shame that the illiterate was unwilling to admit his deficiency to even his closest friend, and so he went stumbling about like a blind man pretending to be able to see.

The Army set up special training camps for these men, camps in which the teaching of reading was a part of the curriculum. Once their defensiveness and feelings of inferiority were overcome, these men showed the eagerness of children to whom new worlds had been opened. They were like blind men who had been offered the gift of vision.

It seems incredible that there should be any question as to the importance of teaching children to read, and indeed it would be difficult to find in print any statement of an educator which raises such a question. Why then has the teaching of reading become an issue?

It appears that the issue has been raised most often by parents who have discovered that their children either cannot read as well as the parents could wish them to or that their children have no wish to read anything other than the funny papers— funny papers which all too often have substituted horror for humor.

We should ask two questions at this point. Has there really been a decline in the effectiveness of the teaching of the three R's, and if there has been a decline, to what can it be attributed?

All too often we jump to the second question without waiting for an answer to the first. The answer to the first question must be somewhat tentative because we have no really accurate records of the achievements in these skills for previous generations, except for very small samples of population. It clearly would be unreasonable to compare the skills of today's children with the skills which their parents possess today as adults of thirty-five or forty-five years. We may safely assume that the parent has done some reading during the past twenty years and that his skills may have improved somewhat since his school years. It is easy for us to forget how little we knew or how poor our skills were when we were twelve. It is by no means certain that adults, even with their greater maturity and subsequent learning, really are better in the elementary skills than are the children in today's schools.

One superintendent of schools, confronted by parents who were critical of their children's spelling, suggested a public spelldown between the parents and their own junior-high-school children. The children agreed with alacrity, but the parents to a man refused to take part. At Coulee Dam, Washington, the parents were more reckless. In an old-fashioned spelling bee held in December, 1952, they were spelled down by the high-school sophomores to the tune of ten to six.

A principal in Seattle recently reported the receipt of a letter from a mother complaining that spelling is not taught today as thoroughly as when she went to school and that her own child continually "mispells" words. The letter was addressed to the "principle." Many of us who studied spelling thirty years ago can sympathize with this mother, but we had better admit that methods of teaching spelling were not infallible in our day either. To paraphrase Will Rogers, "The schools ain't what they used to be and probably never was."

Some scattered evidence is available from objective tests of reading, arithmetic, and spelling which have been given to children over the years. Most of these cover only a ten- or fifteen-year span, but in a few cases they cover as much as a generation, and in one or two instances tests which were given as long as fifty years ago have been repeated with present-day children. In nearly all of these instances the children of today compare favorably with those of bygone years.

In some cases the results are distinctly favorable to the children of the present day; in others there is little evidence of significant change; in only a very few cases does the evidence show any real decline in these skills.

But some of us are convinced that teaching these things just as well as we did in 1920 or in 1900 is not nearly good enough. We ought to be teaching them far better if our increased knowledge of the psychology of learning has been of any use to us. And when a parent protests that Junior cannot read, it does not comfort him to be told that the *average* child reads as well as did his grandparents. Junior still cannot read, and the parent will understandably remain unhappy until something is done about it.

Even if we can agree that the three R's are and will continue to be essential skills, the problem of deciding upon the fundamental objectives remains with us. The determination of objectives is a matter of basic policy, and in a democracy such policy must be decided upon, or at least approved, by the people.

The well-educated teacher ought to have some definite opinions on this subject and should understand the philosophical implications of his choices. But all too often a frill is, to the teacher, what the other fellow teaches. To the football coach Latin seems frivolous; the specialist in Caesar's *Gallic Wars* regards football as a passing fad and hopes wistfully that it will hurry up and pass.

If the superintendent of Mr. Troutstream's school had possessed a clear understanding of the educational objectives of his school, he would have been able to say at the beginning that fishing was not the most effective method of attaining those objectives. Lacking such an understanding, he found himself unable to discriminate between the important and the trivial.

# CHAPTER X

# HICKORY STICKS: THE PROBLEM
# OF DISCIPLINE

The hickory stick has all but disappeared from the American classroom and there are few to mourn its passing. Occasionally an irate citizen, whose petunias have been trampled by little feet taking short cuts on the way home from school or whose expensive bay window has been shattered by a wayward baseball, recommends its reinstatement. And now and then one hears from an unreconstructed Hoosier Schoolmaster who at the close of a trying day has a nostalgic wish to return to the time when he could express his opinion of the growing child with something more than a tired smile. Most of us, however, are willing to say good riddance.

But if the rod is fast becoming a museum piece, progressive educators can take little credit for its demise. The forces which led to that demise were gaining impetus long before the appearance of John Dewey on the educational scene. Most important of these forces was the growing humanitarianism which first made itself felt in the late eighteenth century, gained ground in the nineteenth, and reached its full development in the early part of the twentieth.

This humanitarianism, which was not limited to America, was reflected in and given impetus by the novels of Charles

Dickens, Harriet Beecher Stowe, and many lesser writers. It led to the abolition of slavery and to the more humane treatment of prisoners, of the mentally defective, and of the insane. It resulted in the improvement of the working conditions of laborers and in the greater freedom of women. It was inevitable that it should eventually occur to someone that children too are people and hence deserving of humane treatment. And while there must always have been many teachers who were humane and considerate of the dignity of the child, there were —and are—petty tyrants in many classrooms.

Any teacher who is at heart a despot has remarkable opportunities to exercise his tyranny. For in matters of classroom discipline the teacher plays a multiple role: he is at once the accuser, prosecutor, jury, judge, and executioner. He is also the lawmaker. With such vast powers it was inevitable that both the profession and the public should find it desirable to establish some controls over him.

Consistent with the American concept of the rights of the individual, such controls have been placed over all who are responsible for the behavior of others. The infantry sergeant has been allowed, at least until very recently, a freedom of invective unknown to those responsible for the development of the minds and the vocabularies of children, but even he is not permitted to strike his men or to beat them with sticks.

But the strongest argument against the use of corporal punishment in the classroom is the effect of such punishment on learning. Its use always arouses violent emotional response not only in the child being punished but also in every child present and surely in the teacher as well. The teacher who can strike a child while remaining calm and unemotional himself is a pretty cold fish.

The creation of such an emotional atmosphere inevitably

stops, or at least seriously interferes with, all learning for a considerable period of time. Maybe not quite all learning, for the punished child may indeed learn to avoid such punishment and will very likely learn to hate the teacher and the school just as an apprentice riveter who was struck by the foreman would learn to hate the foreman and construction work in general. Children, and particularly adolescents, are not really so much different from adults in this regard, and it is dangerous to assume even that they get over these insults more rapidly than do adults. Many a child has carried a hatred of a teacher well into his adult life, sometimes a hatred based upon just one incident in which he felt himself to have been treated unfairly or punished too severely. The fact that a few people report that they greatly respected and even liked the teachers who beat them does not mean that many of us are so thick-skinned.

But while the paddled child may learn some things through his experience, it is unlikely that for the next half hour or longer after punishment, he will learn very much arithmetic or algebra or that he will increase his understanding of lyric poetry or Jeffersonian democracy. Such learning is a highly organized activity, and strong emotion is essentially disorganized and disorganizing. The child whose adrenals are secreting freely is like the man in Stephen Leacock's story who jumped on his horse and rode off in all directions. One cannot very well be highly organized and disorganized at the same time, and so the angry or frightened child is not likely, during the period of extreme emotion, to accomplish much learning of an intellectual nature.

II

Although the hickory stick is going the way of the rack and the lash, the problem of discipline is ever with us. It is unfortunate that the concept of school discipline has become confused, in the minds of many, with the idea of corporal punishment. The school can do very well without such punishment, but neither the school nor the society in which it exists can maintain itself without discipline. Dictionaries give at least six definitions for the word "discipline" used as a noun and three more used as a verb. When the critic complains that today's school does not have enough discipline, it is not always easy to discover just what definition he is using. But it appears that most often he is referring to the definition of discipline as "training with a view to right conduct and to prompt and effective action."

It seems clear that today's youth are by no means incapable of such discipline nor are they, in all circumstances, without it. Students in a good school orchestra or choir are excellently disciplined. And there is no better example of a well-disciplined body of men than that of a well-coached football team. The members of such a team are surely trained for prompt and effective action. They rarely refuse to accept the orders of the coach, the captain, or the quarterback and to carry out such orders with dispatch and energy. When a decision of the officials goes against them they may give vent to a burst of anger, but it is most unusual for them to dispute the decision for long, even if they are certain that it is erroneous. In carrying out the orders of their leaders they willingly risk injury and ignore pain and fatigue. And even the most hard-boiled coach is usually more respected by these boys than is the mellower academic teacher who is reluctant to demand anything really difficult of them.

Of course there is some room for doubt that the objectives of football are such as to justify all this expenditure of energy, and at best the advantages of football discipline are available only to those few of our adolescents who are fortunately endowed physically. At any rate here is excellent proof that the young people of today can be disciplined. And it is interesting to note that these examples of good discipline fall within the realm of the much-criticized extracurricular activities.

It would be comforting to be able to report that the discipline of the gridiron carries over to other aspects of the boy's life, that the disciplined athlete shows the same discipline in his attack upon a problem in geometry or the mowing of the lawn at home. It would be reassuring to point out that his respect for his coach and for the referee carries over to a respect for parents, employers, and policemen.

Unfortunately there seems to be little evidence of any such transfer. The halfback who seems so well disciplined on a Saturday afternoon gives way easily to fatigue when asked to weed the garden, ignores his father's sage advice, and is rude to his Aunt Nellie. This evidence of a lack of transfer seems to be confirmed by the findings of research psychologists who report that character traits are, in the main, specific to the situation. Even habits of honesty do not carry over very well from one situation to another. A man may be scrupulously honest in his financial dealings and yet lie under oath in traffic court. This is most unfortunate and makes the teaching of character much harder than it would otherwise be but the evidence for it is pretty firm. This being the case, the parent should be cautious about blaming the school for the child's lack of discipline at home. If the child is undisciplined at home, it is very probable that the fault lies with the home training rather than with the school. But if the schoolroom itself is undisciplined, the teachers and the school administrators must accept much of the responsibility.

## III

What is a properly disciplined classroom? There are few thoughtful adults today, either parents or teachers, who think that the ideal classroom is a place of rigid order. Learning is an active process. If the learning is physical, or muscular, the activity must be physical; if the learning is intellectual, or symbolic, the activity must be intellectual—it must involve the manipulation of symbols. Many psychologists prefer to make no sharp distinction between the terms "physical" and "mental," but at any rate it is necessary to distinguish between large-muscle activity and that which does not involve the large muscles.

Learning also involves some degree of freedom of choice, and this is particularly true of that learning which is a preparation for living in a free society. The citizen in a democracy must learn to make wise decisions; obvious examples are the decisions which he makes as a member of a jury and as a voter.

The citizen must learn to live within the rules. As a citizen in a democracy he may alter the rules through established processes, but until the rule is changed he is responsible for its observance. Though some progressive educators have denied it, it seems clear to most of us that the school must be, in part, a preparation for adult life. If this is true, it follows that the school in a democracy should prepare the child first to live comfortably and effectively within the rules and later to take his part as a citizen in changing those rules which need to be changed. As he reaches his adolescent years he should learn the principles of democracy by taking a greater part in the making of the rules; but he cannot yet make them all because he is not yet fully mature, and because the school exists within the framework of a larger society.

A comparison with football again seems appropriate. Any of the rules may be changed, and indeed the rules are changed from time to time. But the high-school player who thinks that five downs would be better than four or that slugging the pass receiver would be less trouble than intercepting the pass quickly learns that the rules may not be changed midway in the season and surely not by any one player. The rules were made for the purpose of carrying out certain objectives; they should be changed only by those who have a clear understanding of those objectives.

A properly disciplined classroom is one in which the rules are reasonable and in which they are so well accepted by the children that violations are comparatively rare. It is not one in which violations frequently occur and are severely punished. No one would define a well-disciplined football game as one in which there are many fifteen-yard penalties and in which half the players are ejected from the game.

The rules appropriate to a classroom are the rules of normal civilized behavior of individuals in a social setting. They involve courtesy and a consideration for others. But they involve too the active and energetic pursuance of a goal. The goals may be somewhat individualized, but there must be also some common factor. This common factor may be the appreciation of poetry, the understanding of the Constitution, or the ability to read. The decisions regarding the common factors and their relative importance cannot be made by the children, particularly by small children, because they have insufficient understanding of the long-term goals. It is doubtful that such decisions should be made entirely by the teachers, for where they enter the field of policy they must be decided upon or approved by the general public.

If it is true that there is a lack of good discipline in many contemporary schools, it seems likely that this lack results in part from our failure to decide upon the goals of education. If the goals are vaguely defined or understood, if the children's goals are different from those of their teachers or different from those intended by their parents, good discipline is impossible.

But some of the lack may properly be attributed to a misinterpretation of psychological, particularly of psychoanalytic, findings. The ideas that discipline is frustrating and that frustration is to be avoided presumably come from Freud's principle that neurosis grows out of frustration. Freud does seem to say that all neurosis has its origin in frustration, but certainly he did not hold that frustration *inevitably* results in neurosis nor that the proper way to educate a child is to arrange for him an artificial environment in which frustrations do not exist. A more understanding application of Freud's principle would involve letting the child meet frustrations while helping him to react to them in such a way as not to become neurotic. The fullback who, on fourth down, is stopped a yard short of the goal line is surely frustrated; but we do not allow him an extra down merely for that reason, and he rarely becomes neurotic as a result.

If by discipline we mean letting the child learn that there are certain restrictions and controls which society places upon the individual and that children are not exempt from these controls, there seems to be no sound psychological reason for avoiding discipline. Indeed, such discipline would seem to be an essential part of education. The writer can think of no psychologist of note who ever proposed letting the child do just as he pleased. Rousseau was not a psychologist, whatever

else he may have been. Indeed, few if any educational philosophers, even those of progressive leanings, would propose such
a thing.

Yet many teachers and some parents believe that they ought
to allow the child complete freedom. Of course they find it
impossible to do so consistently, and in their confusion and
their failure they often react by becoming more harsh than
teachers and parents of the past.

# CHAPTER XI

# ACADEMIC AND OTHER FREEDOMS

Questions of academic freedom have most often been raised in connection with the colleges and universities. But the current controversy over public education has increasingly brought these questions to the attention of the secondary school, and even the elementary school is by no means unaffected by them.

It is unfortunate that many teachers, as well as the critics of teachers, think of academic freedom strictly in terms of the rights of the teachers themselves. This has led a few teachers to think that such freedom includes the right of the teacher to give his allegiance to an organization dedicated to the overthrow of free institutions. And it has led some of the critics to the conviction that academic freedom is the last refuge of the academic scoundrel.

We will be on much firmer ground if we state our definition in terms of the learner. Academic freedom is freedom of the learner to seek the truth. The corollary is that the teacher must be free, first to seek the truth, and then to make use of the truth, or the best approximation to it available to him, in his teaching. He must have this freedom, not as a matter of his own personal rights, but because the student cannot be really free in his search for truth unless the teacher shares his freedom.

As a citizen the teacher has the same rights, privileges, and responsibilities as has any other citizen. In his personal life he is entitled to the same freedoms as is the lawyer, the physician, the banker, or the farmer. If a teacher is prohibited activities which are permitted other responsible citizens in his community, he has every right to protest, but on the grounds of his *personal*, not his academic freedom.

"Teaching" has at least three fairly distinct meanings: (1) It refers to the teacher's part in the development of the skills of the student. (2) It sometimes refers to a conscious effort to persuade or to convince the learner of the correctness or the desirability of a point of view or of a course of action. (3) Most important of all, it refers to the assistance which the teacher gives the student in his search for truth, to the teacher's role in imparting and clarifying knowledge.

Academic freedom has to do with only the third of these definitions. No teacher can reasonably expect to be free to teach children those skills, the employment of which is prohibited in our society. He may not, for example, teach them to pick pockets. Nor can the teacher be free to promulgate a point of view or advocate a course of action which is antithetical to our laws or our mores. He may not, in our society, attempt to convince young people that homosexual activity is desirable. If he teaches in a parochial school he is not permitted to be an evangelist for some church other than that which supports the school. And if he teaches in a state-supported school it seems reasonable to most of us that he should not be a propagandist for political beliefs which would lead to the overthrow of his own form of government.

But the teacher should insist upon the right of the mature student to seek the truth about sex, about the various religions and their role in history, and about conflicting political doctrines. And he should insist upon his right as a teacher to assist the student in his search for the truth. In this search the student may properly read from the writings of Plato, Hobbes, Nietzsche, and Marx, all of whom proposed forms of government which may be described as "un-American." The child who grows up without a knowledge of communism and of fascism will be woefully unprepared for his responsibilities as an adult citizen and a voter because he will be unable to recognize communistic and fascistic tendencies when they crop up within our own country under some other name.

Academic freedom, defined as freedom to seek and to teach the truth, is absolutely essential to education in a free society. Without it the school becomes merely a propaganda agency for whatever group imposes the limits upon its freedom. Every authoritarian government finds it necessary to impose strict limits upon what the student may learn because no tyrant can face his subjects or remain secure upon his pedestal if his subjects learn the truth.

A truly representative government, on the other hand, can well do without such limitations, indeed it can flourish only if such limitations are not imposed. In a democracy the efforts to restrict the freedom to learn the truth have come most often not from governmental leaders but from special-interest groups within the country. In the history of the United States many such groups have attempted to limit the freedom to learn and to teach. These attempted limitations have most often been concerned with areas of knowledge in which truth is least certain, in which there is honest disagreement as to what is verifiable.

Though in earlier centuries such men as Galileo and Copernicus encountered difficulties with the authorities, the astronomer or physicist today is rarely hampered in his research or teaching so long as he limits himself to his field of expertness and keeps clear of politics. But the biologist has occasionally met with opposition from groups whose concept of the truth about the origin of species differs from his own interpretation; in such fields as economics, sociology, and political science there is a long history of attempts to say what the teacher may and may not teach—of attempts to inhibit his search for the truth.

Occasionally the special-interest group admits to a conviction that the truth itself is dangerous, but more often its objection is to the teaching of something which it is convinced is *not* the truth. Sometimes such a group succeeds in establishing its view as law. The people of Tennessee a generation ago objected to the teaching of the principles of evolution, not because they feared the truth but because they were convinced that these principles were false. The quarrel here was between a group of teachers who were convinced that they had ample evidence, both empirical and rational, to sustain the theory of evolution as truth and a group of citizens who were either unfamiliar with this evidence or who were convinced that their own authoritative doctrine was more reliable than was the evidence of the biologists. It is all too easy to laugh away this problem by saying that the citizens of Tennessee were backward or unenlightened, but the problem is a real one and is ever with us. Yesterday it was biology; today it is economics and politics; tomorrow it may well be something else.

Some teachers have tried to avoid this dilemma of determining what is truth by declaring that they present only the facts in each case and let each child draw the conclusions for himself. But this rarely satisfies the critic who rightly suspects that the teacher cannot present *all* the evidence and that he will select evidence on the basis of the conclusions which he himself has drawn.

There is no simple answer to this problem of presenting the truth in areas in which truth is highly debatable, and probably there is not even a complex answer which will satisfy all parties. But we can reasonably expect that the teacher will make every effort to be fair, that while presenting the facts he will try to avoid indoctrination, at least in those areas in which there is widespread disagreement. We can reasonably ask that in cases in which the child comes to school with beliefs which are contrary to the evidence generally accepted by educated people the teacher will proceed with caution and good judgment and will avoid the emotional upset which results from a sudden kicking of the props from under the child's beliefs. If children enter the first grade with a firm belief in Santa Claus, the good teacher will not insist upon his rights to debunk Santa Claus on the opening day of school.

Those teachers who are concerned with the areas of knowledge most intimately related to this struggle for freedom, the areas of the social studies and the humanities, face a grave problem, the problem of determining the part which the schools should play in this struggle. Some have assumed that the position of the schools should be one of neutrality, though no one has been entirely clear as to just what neutrality involves. Does it involve the presentation of the facts about the various political systems in such a way as to imply that they are of equal merit? Does it mean letting an exponent of each of the various points of view defend his system and then allowing each child to decide for himself? Or does it mean neutrality only in those areas in which we are not already committed by the Constitution of the United States? Teachers have been uncertain and in their uncertainty have made themselves vulnerable to attacks from all sides.

One group of educational leaders chose not to be neutral. In the tumultuous period of the early thirties when it seemed to many that our entire economic system was threatened with convulsive breakdown, this group, which was small but vocal, called upon the teachers to recognize the corporate and inter-dependent character of the contemporary order and to take the lead in transferring the democratic tradition from indi-vidualistic to collectivist economic foundations. These leaders proposed a fundamental remaking of our economic system, and a few went so far as to urge teachers to adopt the concept of the class struggle as their guide, to identify themselves with the working class, and to strive vigorously to make the public school an instrument in the creating of a new social order in which the welfare of the working class would be the primary consideration. Though these proposals were couched in terms designed to make them appear a natural extension of American ideals, their similarity to Marxist doctrine could not be ignored, and this similarity gave impetus to the charge that Communists were trying to take control of the schools.

Members of this group identified themselves as progressive educators, but their proposals were repudiated by Dewey and by many other educators who had regarded themselves as progressive. As so often happens, however, the repudiations received less attention than the proposals, and a great many citizens, including some teachers, assumed these proposals to be an integral part of the progressive point of view. Many of the current attacks upon the schools are based at least in part upon the writings of this small group. It is only fair to say that some of these same educators have made it very clear in their more recent writings that they are vigorously opposed to the development of communism in America, but the damage which they did to the public's confidence in the schools was enormous and is still in evidence. And the violent, though understandable public reaction has made teachers, particularly teachers of the social studies, unduly timorous about taking a firm stand on anything.

These proposals, made in 1933 and 1934, must be evaluated in terms of the confusions which existed in those unhappy years. But from our vantage point of 1953 it seems clear, as Frederick Lewis Allen has so well pointed out, that we in America are evolving not toward socialism or communism but past them. We have our own American economic system, and it is something new in the world—so new that we do not have a satisfactory name for it. It is not capitalism in the old sense, but neither is it socialism. It makes room for free enterprise but also for powerful labor unions, and for a good deal of governmental planning. But despite the extension of government, the government is the umpire more often than the owner.

Despite all our unsolved problems our economic system is today working so well that other nations, socialist, communist, and fascist, are coming to us for aid and we are able to help them all. With 6 per cent of the world's population, we produce about one half of all the world's manufactured goods, and these goods are now being distributed far more equitably than they were a half century ago. Though we still have our poor, the economic level of the American worker is the envy of the world.

Twenty years ago many people thought that collectivism in some one of its many forms was the wave of the future. Many teachers as well as others who thought of themselves as liberals made the tragic error of confusing such concepts as class struggle and the left with liberalism and even with democracy. Today there are those among us who still think of communism, even as it is practiced in Russia, as an extreme form of liberalism, though if these people have any real knowledge of recent history they can hardly be regarded as rational beings. Tyranny over the minds of men, whatever form it may take, is the antithesis of liberalism.

There is an unfortunate and confused tendency on the part of many Americans to think of political ideologies as being ranged along a straight line with fascism at the right and communism at the left. Teachers were among the first Americans to recognize the dangers to us which were inherent in the political systems represented by Mussolini and Hitler, and to many it seemed to follow that in backing away from fascism we must go toward the left, toward communism. This confusion led some sincere liberals during the Spanish Civil War to side with the Republicans, not so much because they liked communism but because they hated fascism. Even today there are liberals in England, as well as in this country, who seem to believe that because they dislike Chiang Kai-shek they must sympathize with the Chinese Communists.

It is a curious fact that our schematic arrangement of political ideologies in 1953 is based upon the seating arrangement in the French National Assembly of 1789. If we will but substitute a triangle for the straight line—a triangle with fascism at one corner, with communism at another, and with democracy at the third—much of this difficulty can be avoided. We then can retreat from fascism and from communism at the same time. No longer will we look upon democracy as a middle position, subject to being pulled or pushed to the left or to the right at the whims of Communists or Fascists. It will have a firm and stable position all its own.

Confronted by the complicated political ideologies of recent years, some well-meaning liberals have been confused and in their confusion have given unwitting support to the enemies of freedom. But they are not the only ones. Many people who are not liberal at all have been equally confused. Their confusion is indicated by their tendency to lump Communists, Socialists, liberals, and intellectuals together and to tar them with the same brush. In so doing they make it far more difficult to identify the real subversives than it ought to be.

When the conservative assumes that in avoiding communism he must retreat to the right—toward fascism—he is making the same mistake as is the liberal who allows himself to be driven toward communism. Both can avoid their confusion by substituting the triangle for the straight line.

There is no room in America for either fascism or communism, but there is plenty of room for a wide variety of opinion which will allow liberals and conservatives to work together under the American system. Democracy is a broad and general term and is subject to numerous and subtle interpretations. The subtleties may be open to debate, but the one basic respect in which democracy differs from communism, from fascism, from absolute monarchy, and from all tyrannies is this: Democracy rests upon the assumption that all rights of the government are derived from the consent of the governed. All men are endowed by their Creator with certain *inalienable* rights. States exist for the welfare of the individual—not the reverse. This is not a scientific fact. It is not subject to empirical verification. It is not so much a fact as it is a statement of values, of a decision which has been made. It is affirmed in the Declaration of Independence and in the Constitution and has many times since been reaffirmed by the American people. The forms which democracy may take may be altered through legal and constitutional procedures, but this fundamental principle cannot be so altered.

On many political issues the American teacher can and should remain neutral, issues upon which the people have not yet come to a decision, issues regarding which there is room for difference of opinion within the framework of democracy. But on the fundamental principles the teacher cannot and should not remain neutral. The decision has been made. The schools in a democracy can and must do everything possible to defend and to promote that democracy. They must uphold the citizens' inalienable rights and must oppose every form of tyranny over the individual.

In his role of citizen the teacher has a right to propose any political changes which can be brought about under the Constitution. In his role of teacher he has the right and duty to assist the student in his search for truth. The first is personal freedom; the second is academic freedom. If teachers continue to cry "academic freedom" in defense of their fellows who have given allegiance to organizations which would eliminate the rights of the individual, there is real danger that they will lose their own freedom to seek the truth. Each issue involving the personal rights of the teacher must be fought out on its own merits, but academic freedom must be upheld as distinct from these issues. Only if this is done can we be certain that the schools will maintain their integrity in the fight for freedom.

II

If parents and teachers can come to some agreement on the nature and importance of academic freedom, the air will be cleared somewhat but it is not likely that such agreement alone will eliminate the charges that the schools are harboring subversives. To understand these charges and to understand the teachers' reaction to them, it will be necessary to go back at least a quarter century, because the older teachers know that such charges have been made for many years.

When I was a sophomore I once was called aside by a citizen

who asked in a whisper if I realized that the college I was attending was a "hotbed of communism, atheism, and free love." I was more amused than startled because the students of my acquaintance included, so far as I was aware, no Communists and very few real atheists. The sexual mores were not always rigidly observed, but love was rarely "free" even under the relaxed moral standards of the late 1920s. I have since heard this same charge made against a great many colleges and more than a few high schools. Such beliefs about our schools seem to have become almost a part of our folkways.

It is true that higher education has occasionally resulted in some changes in the religious beliefs of the students. But it must be said that if the schools have ever taught communism or free love their teachings have been remarkably ineffective if we are to judge by the behavior of the graduates and by the beliefs which they hold.

A survey of college graduates made in 1951 by *Time* and published in *They Went to College* (Harcourt, Brace and Company, Inc., New York, 1952) offers some interesting data on this subject, and it would be well to keep in mind that these college graduates were, for the most part, the products of our public elementary and high schools as well as of the colleges. The *Time* survey revealed that 99½ per cent of all graduates vote for either Democratic or Republican candidates. Some of these graduates list themselves as independents, but this merely means that they feel free to shift back and forth between the major parties. Only 0.5 per cent vote for any of the minor parties, so that the number who vote communist must be only a fraction of this last percentage.

The survey did not take a direct poll of the number of atheists, but 91 per cent of the Catholic graduates and 84 per cent of the Protestant graduates flatly disagreed with the statement,

"Religion has little to offer intelligent, scientific people today." Surely all atheists and most agnostics as well would have agreed with the statement.

Nor did *Time* attempt to estimate the amount of free love among college graduates. But the survey did reveal that the graduate is every bit as likely to marry as is the nongraduate, and once married he is more likely to continue living with his first spouse.

In recent years charges of free love in our schools and colleges have become less frequent, and accusations of atheism have been replaced by charges that the schools promote secularism. But the charges that the schools are communistic or that teachers are "teaching communism" have increased in both frequency and vigor.

This should not surprise us, for international communism has become a very real threat both internally and externally, a threat which no citizen can safely ignore or laugh off. There seems little doubt that Communists have gained entrance into strategic positions in our nation because we have court evidence of their presence in governmental positions and strategic research organizations and there can be little doubt that some have found their way into education.

But charges that the schools are teaching communism have been made so frequently, so loosely, and for so long that teachers have become skeptical of all such accusations. The teachers know that in a great many cases such charges have been totally erroneous and have done great harm to blameless individuals. They know that children, particularly adolescents, often misquote their teachers, sometimes through misunderstanding and sometimes in an effort to shock their parents or to gain a point in a family argument. They know that the adolescent is in the process of establishing his intellectual and emotional independence from his elders and often seems to enjoy taking the side of any question which is contrary to that of his parents. In so doing he takes an unorthodox point of view, and the parent may assume that this point of view is learned at school.

If teaching communism means teaching the facts about communism, it is difficult to see how an intelligent and thoughtful adult can object. The one who does object will logically be forced to object to the teaching of facts about cancer since surely no one approves of cancer.

When the teacher is accused of teaching communism what is usually meant is that someone suspects him of trying to lead children to accept communist principles. But when the accused teacher is defended by other teachers, the defenders mean to imply only that they must be free to teach the facts. So long as teachers and critics continue using different definitions of teaching, just so long will they continue to misunderstand each other.

When teachers are unjustly accused, other teachers can and must defend them, as should every other good citizen. When charges are made, and not yet proved, the right to a fair hearing must be insisted upon. If this is not done, teachers will become so timid about dealing with anything controversial that they will lose their effectiveness as teachers. But this tendency of teachers to rush to the defense of their colleagues who are accused of communistic leanings has led many citizens to believe that teachers as a group are not loyal Americans. In the struggle of the free world against totalitarianism, the teachers have failed to make their own position clear. They seem, to the public, to have taken a fuzzily construed intermediate position, though the recent policy statements of several organizations of teachers and educational leaders should make for clarification.

I think it is an unquestionable fact that the great majority of teachers hate communism and love the free institutions of the United States as much as do politicians, plumbers, businessmen, or lawyers. They know that under communism there would be no such thing as academic freedom. Why then have they delayed making their position clear?

The explanation is a complicated one. It lies in the intellectual history of the twenties, the thirties, and the early forties. During this period the intellectuals came to be suspicious of anything like a protestation of loyalty; they learned to hate chauvinism and to be somewhat contemptuous of flag waving and of open declarations of patriotism. Perhaps they read too much Mencken, but one cynic can hardly be blamed for anything so widespread. In part they were reacting to the disillusionment which followed World War I.

Today most older teachers will admit that this mood of yesteryear seems somewhat adolescent. The leaders of the Veterans of Future Wars became good soldiers and real veterans. Those who had once been tolerant of European tyrannies or had said that these threats to freedom were none of our business were forced to the conclusion that freedom is indivisible and well worth fighting for.

In their own minds most teachers have taken a stand. They hate all tyrannies and few can now deny that communism leads to tyranny. Though they still dislike flag waving, they know that democracy must be defended. Why do they not say so clearly and emphatically?

Perhaps it is because they are afraid; afraid that in meeting attacks from the left they will be driven to the right; afraid of being chauvinistic; afraid of identifying themselves with the witch hunters or afraid that they will stand in the way of progress. To some these will seem curious things to fear, but not to those who grew up in and remember the mood of the twenties and the thirties.

Those fearful of communism in the schools should be encouraged by the fact that both leading teachers' organizations, the National Education Association and the American Federation of Teachers, have voted overwhelmingly that Communists should not be teachers and that proof of membership in the Communist party is good and sufficient reason for debarring a teacher from the profession.

Unfortunately such proof is not easily found. In the search for it there is danger that many loyal teachers will be frightened into ineffectiveness because teachers are peculiarly vulnerable. It is an occupational disease, or an occupational requirement, that they talk a great deal. A high-school or college teacher of history often utters 10,000 or more words a day—many million words a year—in his classes. Obviously he cannot plan with care everything which he is to say.

An editorial writer or newspaper columnist with his daily stint of two or three hundred words can go over his output with care to make sure that he has said nothing which can be used against him. The minister with his weekly sermon or the senator with his occasional speech can write everything out in advance, but the teacher has no time for such precautions. Much that he says is "off the cuff," and he knows that if he is quoted out of context he can be proved guilty of almost anything in the course of a year, particularly if the quotations are slightly distorted by the children who carry them home. It should not surprise us that teachers, even innocent and completely loyal teachers, do not relish being investigated.

Investigators who are looking for subversive teachers can do much to allay the fears of loyal teachers if they will make clear in advance that they recognize these difficulties which the teacher faces and that they do not plan to accuse a teacher of anything on the basis of random remarks quoted out of context. If they make it clear that they are looking for solid evidence of real disloyalty, most teachers will be glad to cooperate. But an investigation of loyalty is bound to be accompanied by a period of fear, distrust, suspicion, and uncertainty, and in such a climate the effectiveness of the work of the school will surely be greatly impaired.

Those who are to investigate must ask themselves whether the advantages to be gained by the investigation are sufficient to offset the harm done. The answer will depend in part upon the effectiveness of Communists or other subversives as propagandists and upon their number. Because of their effective organization and their fanatical discipline even a few party members may offer a serious threat, but only if these few are in positions of leadership or potential leadership.

How many of the teachers in the schools of America are members of the Communist party? The figures are hard to come by and we have no way of verifying those that are available. The largest estimate I have seen is that of a witness testifying before a Senate subcommittee who was quoted in the press as saying that in 1944 there were about 1,500 cardcarrying Communists among the nation's teachers and that 1,000 of these were teachers in the City of New York.

It is generally believed that the Communist party in the United States has lost a large part of its membership since 1944. If the estimate of the number in 1944 is accepted as accurate it may be that New York City presents a special problem but the five hundred Communist teachers outside that city must be spread very thin; it seems unlikely that they will become a dominant force in education particularly if the noncommunist teachers—over a million of them—are alert to the danger.

Eternal vigilance is the price of freedom, and educational groups must be vigilant just as must the labor unions and the State Department. In rendering our enemies ineffective we must take care not to destroy our own liberties and not to lose the freedom of inquiry essential to education in a democracy. But it is time for us teachers to recognize that the fight against communism is not all witch hunting. Witches are imaginary— Communists are all too real. We must learn to discriminate between the investigation that calls an innocent man a Communist and the one that calls a Communist a Communist.

# CHAPTER XII

# FREE ENTERPRISE AND THE TEACHER

Among American businessmen it is widely believed that teachers in our public schools do not show and do not impart to their students any great respect and admiration for the American system of free enterprise. This belief is probably justified. It is not that teachers are, in any large numbers, subversive or that they are particularly unhappy about the American way of life. But they find it difficult to become excited about the free enterprise system because they are not a part of it in any really vital sense, even though their incomes are derived indirectly from it.

The obvious fact is that public education in the United States is, and for a long time has been, socialized in just the sense that medicine is now socialized in Great Britain. A socialized profession is one in which the members of the profession are employed, controlled, and paid by the state rather than by private individuals or groups, and this description surely applies to the teachers in the American public schools. A usual, but by no means certain, result of the socialization of a profession is that sharp limitations are placed upon incomes. This is one of the factors that physicians in this country fear most because they seem convinced that a limitation on income, an income paid by the state rather than by the client, would result in inferior professional services.

The teacher, as distinct from the physician, accepts the socialization of his profession as necessary and probably inevitable, but he is all too well aware of the deadening influence of the resultant limitation on salary, of its destructive effects on motivation, of its tendency to place the mediocre and the outstanding on exactly the same financial plane. The teacher finds himself trapped in what is called a salary schedule which is, in most cases, based entirely on length of service and formal education. If he is a teacher in the public schools, he will automatically receive the top salary as soon as he has taught for twelve or fourteen years and has his master's degree. Securing this degree is somewhat laborious but, in most universities, not particularly difficult for anyone bright enough to be a teacher in the first place; getting the experience is just a matter of hanging on.

Unless his teaching is conspicuously bad or unless he violates the mores of the community, hanging on is not too difficult in this period of teacher shortages. So he may reasonably expect that by the time he is forty he will arrive at the top of his salary schedule and will continue on the same salary until he retires at sixty-five. He knows that if he becomes a truly great teacher his income will be no more than it will be if he just barely gets by. In either case his top salary, if he teaches in one of the larger or more wealthy cities, will be five or six thousand dollars a year. If he teaches in an average community, it will be four thousand dollars or less—in many cases much less.

To expect the man in such a predicament to feel great enthusiasm for the system of free enterprise is expecting a great deal of human nature. Of course a few teachers can increase their incomes slightly by becoming principals, but this is no solution to the problem of securing better teachers; when they become principals they cease to be teachers.

At this point the businessman will perhaps interject that the teacher, like the minister, renounces worldly goods when he chooses his profession, that he should work for the love of the work and should get his satisfaction from the knowledge that he is contributing to the welfare of mankind. Maybe so in Europe in the Middle Ages, but in the United States as of 1953 this is mostly nonsense. There might be some point to the argument if we could find enough teachers highly devoted to the cause of education—and if they were all bachelors. But the simple fact is that most teachers are pretty normal human beings who are living in the same economic environment as are businessmen, tradesmen, and laborers, and it is probably best that this should be so. They have the same desire for new automobiles and fly rods as does the man next door. Their wives have the same interest in pretty clothes, attractive homes, and laborsaving gadgets as does the wife of the plumber or the grocer. Their daughters want the same cashmere sweaters and their sons the same bicycles and baseball gloves as do the businessman's children. Under these circumstances the teacher who can renounce worldly goods is a pretty odd character because all of these things cost money, the same kind of money which is so useful to the businessman. As a result of all these pressures, teachers, particularly the more able teachers, are leaving the classrooms in droves.

It would at first appear that the solution might lie in a merit system which would make possible higher salaries for outstanding teachers. But when I made such a proposal in a magazine article addressed to businessmen and school-board members, I found my ideas sharply criticized by some of the teachers' organizations. This despite the fact that my proposals were for higher average salaries, higher top salaries, and no lowering of salaries at any level.

It appears that many teachers fear any type of merit system which is based upon anything other than length of service and formal education. There is some basis for this fear because merit systems have in the past been based all too often upon the ratings of principals, and these ratings have sometimes been based upon prejudice or political considerations rather than upon competence in teaching. Some of the organizations of teachers have taken the stand that quality of teaching cannot be measured, that "there is no yardstick for measuring in dollars how much better one teacher is than another."

But the present salary schedules seem to indicate that we have such a yardstick. They clearly imply that a teacher with nine years' experience is better than one with eight years' experience and that one with five years of college is better than one with four years, or perhaps the implication is that the older teacher and the one who has spent more on his education needs more money.

We are confronted here with one of the basic dilemmas of our economic system. Shall we distribute incomes on the basis of need or upon the basis of contribution to society? Both systems exist in the United States, and we seem to be moving gradually in the direction of distribution according to need. All welfare programs are based upon such distribution, but so is the established custom of paying military personnel housing allowances or giving bonuses for dependents.

When the teacher asks for a larger salary because he cannot support his family on his present income, the implication is that salaries should be based on need. When the principal asks higher salaries for his teachers to prevent their leaving the profession for more remunerative employment, the implication is that salaries should be based upon supply and demand or upon the need of society to keep good teachers.

We live in a nation of great wealth, and in such a nation it seems reasonable to most of us that minimum incomes for all people should be sufficient to provide a decent standard of living. But what of the maximum incomes? These, it seems, should be based upon contributions to society which are over and above the minimum requirements.

In most cities, if teachers are to have a maximum income of four to six thousand dollars and other professions are to have a maximum income of many times that amount, it is inevitable that the most able of our young people will gravitate toward the other professions, leaving teaching to the less enterprising. But the schools cannot afford to lose these able people. If we are to hold them we need in every school system some opportunities for salaries at least in the ten-thousand-dollar range, and this is still well below the income of the top members of other professional groups. These high salaries for outstanding teachers should not be paid at the expense of other teachers; consequently they will involve some increase in the school budget, but the increase need not be great.

The problem of selecting the superior teachers is indeed a difficult one but we need not be overwhelmed by the difficulty. If one of the endowed research organizations will devote some time and money to the problem, it seems likely that we can develop a merit system at least as effective as those now in use in industry and in the civil service. Merit ratings need not be and should not be based entirely on the judgments of the principal. If the ratings are given a broader and a firmer base, I think that the opposition of the teachers may disappear. Surely teachers do not object to true merit or to the giving of rewards for outstanding teaching; they object only to merit ratings which they consider unreliable or biased.

The details may be worked out by a committee of teachers, a committee to be selected by all the teachers. If this is done and if it is made clear that no teacher's salary will be reduced in order to provide for the higher salaries, it seems likely that teachers will come to welcome the new plan with its incentive to better teaching.

The fact that a merit system can be made to work with teachers has been demonstrated in a great many colleges and universities. Some of the largest universities pay their instructors as little as is paid to beginning teachers in the public schools. But the universities have much less trouble in attracting able people because they offer a real opportunity for advancement to the individual who demonstrates his superior ability. The instructor can advance through the various professorial ranks to the endowed chairs which pay good salaries and carry a great deal of prestige. In the colleges and universities these promotions are not made upon the basis of degrees and years of experience alone as in the public schools. The deans make their recommendations, but judgments are made as well by the professor's colleagues, and in many places the students are now asked to make anonymous judgments of the teacher's effectiveness. It has been found that students can easily tell the difference between an instructor who strives merely to be popular and the instructor who teaches well. Possibly some of these same practices could be adopted in the high school.

There are still many universities which promote faculty members on the basis of research and publications exclusively, and of course such a practice would not be appropriate in the public school where teaching effectiveness must be the criterion. But if the colleges can differentiate the average and the outstanding teacher, as some do, the public schools should find such differentiation no more difficult. Obviously the selection will be based, to a considerable extent, upon a distillation of subjective judgments, and there will always be a possibility of error. There is the same possibility of error as is found in the selection of an officer to command a regiment, in the choice of a president for a corporation, or of the chief surgeon in a hospital. But no one suggests that such leaders should not be selected merely because of the possibility of error.

Probably our proposals are much too modest. In a large school system there ought to be, if we really believe in an economy based upon the motivational effects of financial rewards, a few classroom teachers whose worth to society is a good deal higher than any figures we have mentioned. And somewhere in the United States there is an individual who is the very best classroom teacher in the country. Is it unreasonable to assume that he ought to be receiving rewards somewhat comparable to those given the best dentist, the best lawyer, the best beer salesman in America? Are his skills and talents less outstanding or less important than those of the others? Under the present system, he is probably receiving a salary smaller than that of an anthracite miner. He is not mentioned in *Who's Who* and is unknown except to the boys and girls who are or have been in his classes. He is, nevertheless, the very best classroom teacher in the United States.

In rebuttal some may suggest that the teacher should expect a smaller salary than an entrepreneur or a salesman because he has greater security. But this ignores the fundamental point. Security has great appeal to the incompetent and holds attraction for the mediocre, but to really able and enterprising men it is of little moment; they are far more interested in opportunity. A salary schedule which provides security with little or no opportunity for advancement will always attract the mediocre and the incompetent. An incentive system will attract and hold teachers of real ability who can contribute notably to building the kind of America we all want.

Obviously those responsible for the schools must consider the cost of an incentive plan because educational costs are high and will continue to rise. But the proportion of the national income which has been expended for the public schools has decreased drastically in recent years. In 1930 when the national income was about seventy-five billion dollars, 3.09 per cent of this income was used for public education. But in 1950 when the national income had risen to an estimated 250 billion dollars, the percentage used for education had declined to 1.84 per cent of the total (Edgar W. Knight, *Fifty Years of American Education*, The Ronald Press Company, New York, 1952, p. 334). This has occurred despite the fact that the percentage of the total population in school has increased considerably. With the recent rise in the birth rate, it is obvious that the proportion of the population which is attending school will continue to rise for many years. It is clear that unless the quality of instruction is reduced—and surely no one can look with favor upon such a reduction—the cost of education will increase with the coming years.

All of us are taxpayers and no one likes to see an increase in the cost of anything involving governmental expenditure. But it does not seem likely that our nation will be forced into bankruptcy by its expenditures for the schools. As a people we still spend as much for tobacco and twice as much for alcoholic beverages as for all public education. Even those of us who are addicted to the weed and who like our cokes flavored with a jigger of rum can admit that these expenditures are a little out of line. Despite isolated examples of wasteful expenditures in education, it seems likely that the percentage of school budgets which are wasted is much smaller than for any other part of governmental expenditures. It is far easier to find examples of waste or even of fraud in those portions of our budgets given to road building, military expenditures, or public welfare than in those given to the schools. In most branches of government there are at least a few individuals whose jobs are sinecures or who are on the payroll with no real job at all. But no teaching job is a sinecure and no teacher is ever idle. The money spent for education is a wise and necessary investment in our future as a nation.

# CHAPTER XIII

# WHAT WE KNOW ABOUT
# HOW WE CAN TEACH

Any system of education must be based upon philosophical assumptions, including assumptions as to the nature of truth and choices as to what is most valuable and most important. But it must also be based upon someone's interpretations of psychological facts, particularly facts relating to the nature of the learning process, to perception, and to motivation.

For the past fifty years and more, several thousand psychologists have devoted themselves to the problem of discovering and verifying psychological facts. Their methods are not satisfactory to all philosophers but they are consistent with the methods and the assumptions which underlie all science. Psychologists assume, as do all scientists, that a fact is an observed relationship which may be verified by other observers and which has been found to have predictive value. It would seem obvious that those who are planning the schools of tomorrow, unless they reject the scientific method altogether, should make every effort to familiarize themselves with the facts which have been discovered and verified, in so far as these facts may provide a basis for education.

The limitations of the scientific method must be kept in mind. Science can never tell us what *should* be done; it can tell us only how it may be done. If the scientist is a physicist, he can tell us how to make an atomic bomb. He cannot, as a scientist, tell us whether it ought to be invented, or how or when it ought to be used. He can give us not ends but means toward ends.

If the scientist is a psychologist, he can tell us what kinds of experience will make the child more aggressive. He cannot, as a psychologist, tell us whether aggressiveness is a desirable trait or whether this trait should be an aim of education. All scientists, but particularly those who attempt to popularize their ideas, now and then forget the limitations of science and tend to pontificate and to make value judgments, forgetting that in making such judgments they have only the same right to opinion as does the nonscientist.

When the value judgments and the opinions have been sorted out, there remain a few facts, a few principles, a few generalizations upon which there is a fair amount of agreement on the part of nearly all who are familiar with the evidence. Various psychologists use somewhat different terminology in stating these principles, but upon the essential ideas there is some agreement. All those who are planning for the schools should be familiar with these principles because they are the nearest we have to firm facts. Stated in the simplest terms possible some of the agreements are these:

1. *Children of Any Given Age Differ Greatly in Their Capacity for Learning.* We are not entirely certain just how much of this difference is based upon inherited structure and how much on the child's experiences. But it is clear that an increase in motivation will not eliminate these differences; a slow-learning child cannot become a fast-learning child through effort alone. It follows that if school children are grouped on the basis of age and if all members of the group

are expected to learn the same things in the same amount of time, some will learn easily, others with difficulty, and some learn not at all.

2. *There Is No Learning without Motivation.* But motivation may be either intrinsic—based upon interest in the learning activity itself—or extrinsic—based upon rewards or punishments.

The interest in solving a puzzle is an example of intrinsic motivation. Another example is the desire to see how an exciting story will turn out.

Rewards may be physical things, but more often are symbols such as grades, an athletic "letter," or a star on the blackboard. Rewards also include such satisfactions as the approval of other children or of adults. The symbolic rewards are probably effective only if they lead to social approval.

Punishment, as the term is used psychologically, includes social disapproval, low grades, scoldings, and feelings of failure, as well as the more obvious physical punishments. Fear of punishment will usually cause an individual to avoid the situation which led to the punishment. A burnt child avoids the fire. But punishment usually causes fear or anger, and such strong emotion interferes with complex or intellectual learning. The child who has experienced a great deal of punishment in connection with arithmetic learns to avoid arithmetic but not to solve arithmetic problems.

Either rewards or interest will facilitate learning, but a combination of the two is more effective than is either alone. An advantage of interest is that such intrinsic motivation tends to perpetuate itself, whereas rewards must be constantly increased to maintain their effectiveness.

(Nothing which occurs in the classroom is motivated half so well as is the activity on a football gridiron. The athlete is motivated not only by his interest in the game but by the approval of adolescents and adults, by publicity in the papers, and at the end of the season he receives a sweater with a letter a foot high which identifies him a block away as a successful athlete. Is it any wonder that boys work harder at football than at Latin?)

3. *Learning Proceeds Most Effectively When Both the Physical Maturity of the Child and His Background of Experience Have Prepared Him for the Learning Which Is to Occur.* This is what is meant by "readiness." It is obvious that the average three-year-old cannot learn to read however hard he may try and however skillful may be his teacher. It is equally true, though less obvious to most people, that many six-year-olds cannot yet learn to read; but a few four-year-olds are ready to learn to read and a few nine-year-olds are not.

4. *Girls of Any Given Age up Through the High-school Period Are Somewhat More Mature Both Physically and Intellectually Than Are Boys of the Same Age.* This fact has been all but ignored by those who make school policy. It would be far more consistent with the facts to place twelve-year-old girls in a classroom with boys of thirteen than to place them with boys of their own age.

5. *The Dislike for a Specific Subject Such as Arithmetic or Grammar Is the Result of the Child's Unpleasant Experiences with That Subject.* Such specific dislikes cannot be inherited. They do interfere seriously with learning, but they can be avoided through more skillful teaching and by presenting materials at the level of difficulty which is appropriate to the child's maturity.

6. *Personality Characteristics Such as Self-confidence, Introversion, or Aggressiveness Are Very Largely Learned as the Result of the Child's Experiences.* This is the case even though

such experiences may have occurred in infancy and may not be recalled by the individual. Such traits change less readily as the child approaches maturity but will continue to alter somewhat throughout life. (Though this principle is generally accepted by psychologists, there are a few anthropologists and physiologists, such as Sheldon of Harvard, who believe there is evidence of an inherited physiological factor which underlies such personality traits.)

Whether or not it does so intentionally, the school inevitably will influence the child's personality development.

7. *Neuroticism, Emotional Instability, or "Nervousness" Is Due in Part to the Individual's Experience with Unresolved Psychological Conflict.* It may or may not have some physiological basis as well, but such instability can surely be increased by further experience with psychological conflict whether or not there is a physiological basis.

Some of the conflicts which may make a child neurotic occur in the school, and the teacher should be aware of these conflicts if he is to avoid contributing to them.

8. *There Is a Small but Positive Correlation among Those Characteristics Usually Considered to Be Desirable.* These characteristics are intelligence, social acceptability, physical and mechanical skills, and verbal skills. Bright children are not on the average inferior in mechanical skills, and dull children are not on the average superior in such skills. The popular opinion to the contrary of this generalization is based upon the natural tendency to give undue attention to exceptional cases. Many careful studies of abilities covering thousands of cases give evidence of this positive correlation; conspicuous among them is Terman's *Genetic Studies of Genius.*

However simple these principles may seem, each of them has

enormous implications for education. None of them can safely be ignored by those who make educational policy. Most of these principles have been discussed elsewhere in this book, but item 2, which has to do with the relation of interest to motivation, calls for additional explanation because the doctrine of interest is basic to progressive education.

The doctrine of interest may be stated simply as the doctrine that an individual learns best and most easily those things in which his interest is greatest. The most critical problem in evaluating this doctrine lies in the difficulty of defining "interest," because this term has no very distinct psychological meaning. In a general way it refers to an attitude which accompanies a state of attention or to a heightened state of anticipation. Speaking in these general terms, it seems clear that interest is conducive to learning. If a student is interested in history he is more receptive to the ideas which he finds in a history book and is more likely to continue reading the book. If he has no interest in poetry he is unlikely to read poetry voluntarily and may not read with much understanding if the reading is required of him. But all too frequently when the child says he is not interested in a topic or a school subject, what he really means is that he has developed a dislike for it. If he says that he finds mathematics dull and uninteresting, his real meaning is that he has learned to fear or to hate it. This is not merely a lack of interest but a positive attitude which has resulted from experiences of discomfort or failure.

Nearly all teachers will agree that interest on the part of the student is invaluable in education. The only controversy over the doctrine of interest grows out of the interpretation of a few extremists in education who have maintained that the curriculum should be constructed on the basis of the child's interests as they are found without any real effort on the part of the

teacher to develop interest where none exists. It is this interpretation which has led to the do-as-you-please or make-your-
own-curriculum school of thought in education. This group
has never had a very large following in actual practice, but
many teachers seem to think that they *ought* to be basing their
teaching upon the interests which the child brings to school
with him.

The fact that these teachers overlook is that the development
of new interests is the job of the teacher, and the development
of new interests is not at all difficult for the competent teacher.
A good elementary teacher can begin with a group of children
who have never heard of biology and who know little or nothing of biological processes, and by a skillful setting of the
stage can develop in the children a tremendous amount of interest in a very short time. A good high-school teacher can do
the same with problems of government or of physics, as can
a college teacher with geological processes or epistemology.
It is not even necessary that the student know what epistemology means when he enters the classroom, and he may never
have considered the problems of knowledge or of truth. I have
seen these interests developed and developed quickly, and so,
no doubt, have you.

So it is utterly fallacious to assume that the curriculum must
be based upon the student's prior interest. It is necessary only
that he be capable of engendering the interest. There can be no
interest without some knowledge, and a curriculum which does
not move ahead of the immediate interests of the class will tend
to stand still rather than move forward.

II

There is a great and ever-widening gulf between the philosophies and practices proposed by the "frontier thinkers" in

education and the beliefs which are held and the practices actually followed by the great mass of American classroom teachers. The leaders have assumed that the reluctance of the teachers to follow their leadership results from the teachers' ignorance or from their reluctance to accept change. They have given little consideration to the possibility that the teachers may exceed them in common sense or that the teachers may take a more realistic view of actual classroom problems.

Caught in the swirling eddies of progressivism, a great many classroom teachers have managed to avoid being swept away. They listen tolerantly to the big-name educators at teachers' conventions but take their enthusiastic outpourings with more than a grain of salt. They read the books of these celebrities with the same skepticism as do the parents. They attend summer school and take the required courses in education but are far more critical of these courses than we professors ever dare admit to ourselves. And is it significant that more of the jokes about progressive education were originated by teachers than by all other citizens combined.

Through the years, American teachers have evolved their own educational philosophy, a philosophy which does not ignore the psychological facts but which is closely related to the folkways and the mores of the American people. This philosophy has never been clearly enunciated, but it might be interesting to attempt to state its tenets in contrast to those of the spokesmen of progressivism.

Column I contains statements of the point of view of capitalized Progressive Education. Some of these are official policy statements of the American Education Fellowship, and the others are from the writings of leading progressives which have been quoted frequently and with approval in progressive publications. (Needless to say, there are probably few progressives who would espouse this platform point by point; it is a synthesis from the writings of some of the leading spokesmen.) Column II states the point of view represented in this book—one which I believe to be shared by a majority of classroom teachers. Of course it is presumptuous for anyone to attempt to speak for the majority of teachers, but let us risk being presumptuous. Perhaps Mr. Gallup or Mr. Roper will follow up with a poll of the teachers themselves.

It will be seen that on some issues there is no great difference of opinion, while on others the disagreements are basic.

| I  The point of view of Progressive Education | II  The point of view of this book |
| --- | --- |
| 1. The schools should dedicate themselves to the "reconstruction of the economic system in the direction of far greater justice and stability than at present." (Some progressives have made it clear that it is their intention that this reconstruction is to come about through democratic processes.) | 1. Decisions regarding the reconstruction of the economic system should be made by all the people through their democratically selected representatives. The schools should assist children in acquiring the information upon which such decisions may be based. |
| 2. The schools should be dedicated to "the establishment of a genuine world order—an order to which national sovereignty is subordinated to world authority." | 2. This, too, is a decision for all the people—not for educators alone. Again the schools should see that children are informed of the issues and the problems. |
| 3. The curriculum should be based upon the interests of the child because the child is motivated to learn only that which interests him. | 3. Interest is essential to learning, but a skillful teacher can lead the child to become interested in almost anything. The curriculum should be based |

| I<br>The point of view of<br>Progressive Education | II<br>The point of view of<br>this book |
|---|---|
| | upon long-range objectives in education, and these objectives should be determined by adults. The immediate interests of small children is not a reliable guide. |
| | (Even in the case of college students, the free elective system—in which the student selected his own curriculum on the basis of his interests—did not contribute to sound education and is being altered in the direction of a curriculum based upon the judgments of more mature people.) |
| 4. Education is growth. | 4. Education is learning. The school is concerned with those aspects of learning which require mature guidance. We think that the concept of growth as used in education is too vague to be very useful. |
| 5. Education is not preparation for life, education *is* life. | 5. The school years represent an important segment of life, but all education should be a preparation for something as well. The elementary school should, as *one* of its several duties, prepare students for the high school, and the high school should prepare for college those students who are to go to college. All schools should, in the |

| I<br>The point of view of<br>Progressive Education | II<br>The point of view of<br>this book |
|---|---|
| | broadest sense, prepare for adult life. |
| 6. Education is a social process. | 6. Some education is social, some is individual in nature and must involve periods of quiet contemplation. |
| 7. The schools of today and of the past have placed too much emphasis on discipline. This overemphasis is deleterious to mental health or emotional adjustment. | 7. If discipline means harsh punishment and the use of autocratic controls we agree with the progressives that such discipline has no place in the classroom. But discipline defined as "training for right conduct and for prompt and effective action" is an essential part of all education. Such discipline contributes to mental health more often than it interferes with it. |
| 8. The natural impulses of children should not be inhibited or suppressed lest children become frustrated and neurotic. | 8. To become a well-adjusted adult in a civilized community, it is necessary for the child to develop many inhibitions and to learn to suppress many natural tendencies in accordance with the customs of his own social group. We think that such inhibitions can be learned without excessive frustrations and without the development of neurotic tendencies. |
| 9. Education should be based upon "the new psychology." | 9. Education should be based upon all available knowledge of the psychology of the child. |

| I<br>The point of view of<br>Progressive Education | II<br>The point of view of<br>this book |
|---|---|
| | (There are several relatively new systems of psychology as well as several older ones.) |
| 10. Education, being the process of growth, is essentially the same process whether the pupil is a small child, an adolescent, or an adult. The principles of progressivism are as appropriate for the college as for the kindergarten. | 10. Despite the continuity of the learning process, the education of an adolescent or an adult is a very different matter from the education of a small child. Methods, techniques, subject matter, and to some extent philosophy must be different. |
| 11. The child learns "by doing." It follows that schools should place much greater emphasis than they now do on observable or overt activity and much less on symbolic, verbal, or intellectual activities. This is true of education at all age levels. | 11. We think that the elementary school must include a great deal of physical activity in its program but that as the child grows older his education should include an increasing proportion of intellectual activity. The more mature and the more intelligent he is, the more important it becomes that the school stress such intellectual activity if he is to realize fully his potentialities. In the upper levels of education, thinking and learning to make sound decisions become paramount. |
| 12. Schools should eliminate competition between children because competition often has unfortunate effects upon children who are unsuccessful in competing. | 12. We should try to avoid the unhappy effects of overemphasis on competition and of early experience with failure. But our children must live in a competitive society, and it is better to |

I
The point of view of
Progressive Education

II
The point of view of
this book

teach them to face the problems of competition calmly than to avoid competition altogether.

13. The school should be "child-centered"; its activities should be based upon the needs of the child.

(In sharp contrast a few progressives have held that the school should be "society-centered"; its activities should be based on the needs of society. These conflicting views have not been reconciled, but both are held by progressive educators.)

13. In planning educational activities the schools should consider the needs and the rights of children, of parents, of teachers, and of all citizens. Neither the needs of the child nor the needs of society should be the exclusive consideration.

Those of us who prefer not to be classified as progressive educators are in full agreement with the progressives on a great many important issues. We agree that the classroom should be a happy place where children enjoy living, and we agree that there has been improvement in this direction in recent years. We agree that the schools should prepare children for living in a democracy and that the influence of the schools should be to reduce and, if possible, to eliminate prejudice against minority groups. We agree that the schools should recognize individual differences and should adjust their programs to the abilities of all the children. We agree that the schools must always be willing to try out new ideas and to reject old methods when they cease to be appropriate.

But we do not share the enthusiasm of the progressives for change just because it is change. We agree rather with G.

Lester Anderson, Dean of Administration at the University of Buffalo, writing in the third *Yearbook of the American Association of Colleges for Teacher Education 1950* (pp. 25–26) who says: "The pragmatic philosophy, not only all-pervasive in education but a part of the warp and woof of our culture, has made it difficult to stabilize the goals of teacher education even for a sufficiently limited period of time for us to agree tentatively on a program. We are so experimentally minded, so constantly grasping for ever newer concepts and procedures, so unsure of what we have done, so fearful of becoming static, so eager to be 'progressive,' so frightened of 'conservative' forces, so enamoured of expansion which seems synonymous with growth, that we are without stability. Do we not seem to be tacitly accepting as wise the policy of not knowing where we are going but being dead certain that we are on our way?"

## III

Throughout this book I have used the term "education" as though it were synonymous with schooling. This is convenient but misleading because we all know that much that is educative occurs outside the school. We know that Abraham Lincoln was an educated man despite his lack of schooling and that few college graduates can, in their writing, approach the style and clarity of the Gettysburg Address. We know that Shakespeare never had a course in playwriting nor Edison one in physics.

When Henry Adams wrote his autobiography, he saw fit to title it *The Education of Henry Adams* despite the fact that only a few pages were devoted to his school years—and of these years he did not speak highly. He regarded his school years of ten to sixteen as "time thrown away." He thought that Harvard "taught little and that ill." The best he could say for his alma mater was that it left the mind "open, free of bias, ignorant of facts, but docile." (Those who accuse the schools of yesteryear of overemphasizing facts, please note.)

Why should anyone bother to attend school at all? The answer seems to be that most of us, who are neither Lincolns nor Shakespeares, will learn a little more and learn it more easily in a good school than elsewhere. The school is a specialized environment designed to facilitate learning—that is all.

It would be presumptuous indeed for the school to assume that it can or should take over the whole of education, and merely thinking up a phrase like "the whole child" makes it none the less presumptuous. A child finds it enjoyable to learn to make mud pies, to climb trees, to go fishing, and to hike and camp in the woods and the hills. But these are essentially exploratory activities, and exploration loses much of its fun and its educational value if a teacher shows us what, how, when, and where to explore. Imagine Tom Sawyer being guided by a teacher who shows him how to build a raft, how to explore caves, and how to camp out! This would be no real American boy but merely a childish edition of an unimaginative tourist on a guided tour.

In those activities which are essentially either exploratory or recreational the "we learn by doing" dictum of the progressives is appropriate. A child learns to climb trees by climbing them; it makes no great difference how he does it so long as he enjoys himself. But the schools had better devote their time to teaching those things which are not easily learned by random activity and which require mature guidance.

CHAPTER XIV

# PARENTS AND TEACHERS

At the dawn of the human era, the first teacher was a parent who tried to facilitate the learning of a child by showing him how to perform some simple act. The first school was a primitive home. Though specialized schools, such as schools for the priesthood, date back at least to the dawn of written history, the common or universal school is of comparatively recent origin.

The school became necessary only when parents realized that they did not have the time, the patience, or the technical skills or knowledge necessary for teaching children all that they needed to know. But when they permitted the establishment of formal schools the parents had no intention of abdicating their responsibilities in favor of the teachers. They intended only that the schools should assist them in teaching those things in which the parents were least skilled, or for which the parent had least time.

If, for the moment, we limit our discussion to the schools of the United States, it appears that the parents in colonial and pioneer days delegated to the teacher the responsibility for specific instructional activities while retaining the right to make decisions about the length of the school term and the school day, the subjects to be taught, and even to a considerable extent the methods of instruction. If the parent-teacher relationship was a partnership, it was clear that the parent was the senior partner. More often the teacher was a mere hireling subject to the will of each individual parent.

As communities, and consequently their schools, grew in size this situation became increasingly untenable. It became necessary to place the responsibility for school policy in the hands of a body smaller and less unwieldy than the entire group of parents. It was thus that the board of education or school board came into existence.

The local school board seems to be distinctly an American institution. In many European nations the schools have long been directed from a central governmental agency with no local control. But in the United States the local school board was for a long time virtually an autonomous body. It selected teachers and made its own decisions about their qualifications. It made all decisions about the construction of the schoolhouse, the textbooks, the curriculum, and the length of the school term. If the harvest was late, the opening of school could be delayed in order that the boys could assist their fathers in getting in the crops. Its members could, and frequently did, visit the schools and question the pupils for the purpose of determining the quality of the instruction which they had received. This local autonomy made for flexibility and for adaptability to the needs of the local community, but it made also for great unevenness in quality of the schools in various communities. In one community the teacher might be a scholarly gentleman and a skillful teacher. In the adjoining community he might be the village half-wit who was appointed to his position because there was no other way for him to become self-supporting and because it was assumed that anyone could teach school. Even as recently as the depression of the 1930s we often heard of teachers who were appointed to their positions not because of their qualifications but because their families were long-time residents of the community and it was felt that the school board owed them jobs.

In a land in which mobility of population was the rule rather than the exception these inequalities were of concern to everyone. If you lived in a community which supported an excellent school you could be assured that your daughter would have an opportunity for a good education. But her future husband might well be a boy from the adjoining community—the one in which the teacher was grossly incompetent. If you were concerned about the education of your future son-in-law, your interest in the schools extended beyond the bounds of the local district.

Eventually it came to be an acknowledged principle that some minimum standards for education must be established on a broader geographical basis, and as of 1953 the basis has come to be the state. At first the state merely set up examinations as a minimum basis for the selection of teachers, and these state requirements were frequently ignored by the local boards of education. Later the states undertook the training of teachers, the financial support of the schools, and the responsibility for deciding upon the curriculum. This latter responsibility sometimes included the selection of textbooks.

In many states the financial support of the schools remained largely in the hands of the local community until about twenty years ago. With the coming of the depression, many communities found themselves totally unable, or perhaps unwilling, to support the schools, and step by step the states took over that responsibility. The usual process was for the state to provide matching funds. These state funds were made available only to those local school systems which satisfied specific requirements set up by some state authority, usually the state department of education. To receive the state matching funds, the local school must employ only teachers holding state certificates, must extend its school term to some specified period, usually thirty-six weeks, and must meet certain curricular requirements. State control followed state support, and within a very short time much of the responsibility for the schools passed from the local community to the state. This development undoubtedly has raised the standards of the schools, but it also removed the control of the schools still farther from the hands of the parents and contributed to the current dissatisfaction and feeling of frustration on the part of the parents.

Even before the period of state control of education, the control was passing from the parents. The extension of universal education upward had resulted in the attraction to the profession of teachers who were, academically at least, far superior to the country school teachers of pioneer days. The parent or the member of a local school board might consider himself qualified to pass on the qualification of a teacher for teaching spelling and simple arithmetic, but he was less confident of his ability to question the high-school teacher on such subjects as literature, geometry, or chemistry. Such judgment of qualifications he left to the principal or the superintendent of schools. These administrative officials, unknown in the days of the one-room country school, came into existence with the development of cities and with the consolidation of rural schools. Their exact responsibility for school policy has never been very clearly established, but to the parent who wishes to bring about some change in the schools, they represent another step in the hierarchy and sometimes another barrier to be surmounted.

School administrators came into existence when the boards

of education found that their task of selecting and supervising teachers and of attending to school properties had become too great for their part-time attention. In some cases the boards delegated the supervision of instruction to the superintendent of schools while retaining the responsibility for building construction and for the financial problems. Even today many boards of education devote almost the entire time of their meetings to problems of finance and of building construction and repair, leaving instructional policy to the administrator. And many a superintendent of schools, remembering acrimonious debates about methods of teaching or educational policy, prefers to keep it that way. One very successful superintendent of my acquaintance says privately that whenever he detects a tendency on the part of a board member to take up an issue of instructional policy, he sees to it that financial problems become so pressing and complex that discussion of the policy matter is indefinitely postponed.

Many an earnest citizen who has sought election to the board of education because of an interest in education itself is frustrated to discover that the board meetings are devoted exclusively to financial matters. This is partly the fault of those businessmen who campaign for election to boards of education with a promise to put the operation of the schools on a business basis. Such a board member *should* be limited to problems of finance. Problems of purchasing material may quite properly be handled on a business basis, but the training of boys and girls in citizenship, in character, and in self-development cannot. Those who wish to take part in the formulation of instructional policy must do so as citizens rather than as businessmen. But citizens surely should have a large part in the development of school policy.

The parent of 1953 who is dissatisfied with the school his

child attends and who wishes to bring about a change finds himself confronted with a vast and unwieldy organization upon which he can make little dent. The day is long past when he can, as an individual parent, go to the teacher and insist on a change. The teacher will reply that school policy is made by the state office, by the office of the city superintendent, by the office of the principal, or by a committee of teachers or of educators—the words do not have identical meaning. The classroom teacher, as an individual, can no more change school policy than can the individual parent. So when a parent is dissatisfied with the school he is at a loss to know what he can or should do. He does not want to be a complaining parent, and often he feels that teachers do not welcome his suggestions. If he joins a parent-teacher organization in the hope that this will be a place in which problems common to the teacher and the parent can be discussed, often he is disappointed. He finds that the first half of the meeting is dominated by a guest speaker who merely reaffirms some of the educational practices already found in the schools rather than examining them critically, and that the latter portion of the meeting is a social hour in which discussion of important school problems is avoided and a great deal of attention is given to the matter of what kind of refreshments shall be served at the next meeting. In his anger and frustration he may find himself turning to one of the groups which have recently organized to attack and criticize the schools with motives which are, to say the least, dubious.

But what else can the troubled parent reasonably do? What can he do if he feels that while most teachers are conscientious and sincere and that the schools are on the whole pretty good, there are, nevertheless, some changes that definitely need to be made? What can he do if he is convinced that his child is not learning some of the basic skills which he will need? What can he do if he feels that the child is not learning good work habits, or that he is failing to get a sense of values, or is acquiring values which the parent considers wrong? What can he do if he feels that the high-school boy or girl is not getting enough vocational training, or that he is getting too much vocational training at the expense of cultural subjects?

There is a great deal that the parent can do. As we have said earlier, the public schools in a democracy belong to the people, and the people can do with them what they will, through their elected representatives. But this is a very serious responsibility and one which should be exercised with caution. The decisions should be made by all the people, not by small pressure groups, nor by the dissatisfied individuals alone. It is obvious that no one parent can go storming into the schoolroom or the principal's office demanding changes and expect to get a very cordial reception. But the parent can examine the evidence with the teachers and with other parents, and together they can give the problem thoughtful consideration. If the majority of people then desire a change, the school will accept the verdict of the people.

Of course, there are some limitations. All decisions must conform to local, state, and national laws and to the state and national constitutions. Any decision which you make about the teaching of religion, or about any type of segregation of children in the schools must obviously so conform. As citizens in a democracy we can, through due process, change the laws and we can, through amendments, change the Constitution, but until changes are made the school must comply with the law.

It should be remembered too that teachers are citizens; as citizens they have every right to take their full part in all discussions and may rightfully, like any other citizen, try to influence the decisions of others. Moreover, the parents will be wise to take full advantage of all the knowledge and all the experience of the teachers who are devoting full time to these problems and have had a great deal of reason and opportunity to think about them. On some matters of broad policy, problems which are essentially ones of value or of what is most worth while, all intelligent opinions are equally worthy of consideration. On other, more technical or professional problems, problems on which we have evidence based upon long experience or research, the judgment of the experienced teachers should carry greater weight. On some of the more difficult professional problems it may be wise to get evidence from the faculty members in teachers colleges and universities. These professors are not all impractical theorists (not that a few *sound* theorists are not needed in education), but many of them have taught in the elementary and high schools and they have in addition accumulated a great deal of evidence about school problems and have given these problems long and careful thought. Like the members of any profession, some of these people are a good deal wiser than others, but wisdom is something you will have to judge for yourself when you listen to what they have to say.

It is on what may be called technical problems that these professional people can be most useful. They have a great deal of information and evidence on such problems as the ways of determining when the individual child can most profitably start learning to read, the best way to teach long division, the problem of whether an understanding of our government is best gained by a separate course in civics or as part of a general social studies course. Of course their opinions and judgments may still be wrong, but it is best not to make a decision until we have heard all the evidence they can give us.

But on some of the problems of determining what is most

important in the school, the parent may well be better qualified to his opinion than are many teachers. An example is the problem of just how much of the school's time, money, and of the energies of teachers and students should be devoted to music and how much to athletics. It seems obvious that the opinion of the music teacher, however honest and unbiased that teacher may try to be, is influenced by his own experience and the concentration of his own training. For him, music has been a vital experience, and he knows that this experience has come only as the result of long hours of hard work in his field. He knows that if any very large part of his time and energies had gone to athletics his musical training would have suffered. Something very similar but in reverse may be said of the athletic coach who was probably a successful athlete himself and is convinced that he would have been less successful if he had spent long hours playing the violin. We all tend to overestimate the importance of the things we understand best and to underestimate the importance of things we know little about.

As an individual parent you may be equally influenced by your own specialized experiences, but the combined judgment of all the parents should be better than that of any one specialist or group of specialists. Merely apportioning equal time to all subjects taught in the schools is no solution because that would leave too little time to do anything adequately. We must decide what is more important and what is less important.

Are the schools taking up too much of the child's after-school and evening time, time which should be spent at home with the family, or is it the duty of the school to provide an extensive program of sports and social activities which will keep the child occupied when he is not in the classroom? Certainly most schools, particularly the high schools, have been moving in the latter direction. But should they continue doing so, or is it better for the child to spend the late afternoons and evenings with his parents and to learn from them the social skills, working habits, and many other things which we and our parents learned at home? This is surely a complicated problem, one that is related to the problem of working mothers, of fathers who have too little time for their children, and to the fact that city children have fewer opportunities for useful work at home than did their rural grandfathers in their youth. But it is, in the long run, a problem for all the people to decide, not one for the teachers alone.

Within recent years there has been increasing evidence that parents and other citizens are accepting more responsibility for their part in making school policy. By far the most significant of all the moves in this direction has been the work of the National Citizens Commission for the Public Schools. This non-profit corporation for the improvement of public education is made up of members who are not professionally identified with education, religion, or politics. The members reflect many different kinds of experience, but they serve as individuals and do not represent any organization or group. The National Citizens Commission was organized in 1949 under the chairmanship of Roy E. Larsen, president of Time, Inc. It set for itself two immediate goals:

1. "To help Americans realize how important our public schools are to our expanding democracy, and
2. to arouse in each community the intelligence and will to improve our public schools."

The National Commission has received financial support from the Carnegie Corporation, the General Education Board, and the New York Community Trust. It is prepared to provide information and assistance to those who wish to set up local citizens committees in their own communities. The National Commission holds that such committees should be initiated locally, and of course it makes no effort to control the work of such local committees.

Local citizens committees for the schools can be appointed by local governmental authorities, by the school board, by the school superintendent, and by civic organizations—or they may be spontaneously organized by their own members. In any case they should represent all possible elements in the community. All economic levels should be represented as well as all political parties, races, and religions; otherwise they are likely to be accused of being pressure groups and may actually develop into such groups. In its handbook, *How Can We Help Get Better Schools?*, the Commission suggests that, "the difference between a good citizens committee and a dangerous pressure group is simply that the citizens' committee takes into account the interests of *all* the people and all the schools in the community, while the pressure group represents the interests of some of the people, who may be working against the interests of others."

The good citizens committee, in addition to being representative of a full cross section of the community, does not attempt to make recommendations until it has examined all the facts. In getting such facts it cooperates fully with the school authorities and continues this cooperation when the time comes to make recommendations. But the citizens committee must maintain its independence of action and must not become merely a spokesman for the current educational policies unless it decides, after careful examination, that the current policies are sound and are in harmony with the wishes of the majority of the people.

In many communities it has been found that committees which are spontaneously organized have distinct advantages over those appointed by existing authorities. Committees appointed by local governmental authorities may feel an obligation to maintain the *status quo* and may not be representative of the entire community. Those appointed by the school board or by the superintendent may find themselves in a difficult position if there is a difference of opinion between the board and the superintendent.

According to the latest reports, over eight thousand citizens committees have been organized, and new ones are coming into existence at the rate of two hundred and fifty a month. A large number of these committees are in communication with the National Citizens Commission. Other groups which wish to establish such contact may write to the National Citizens Commission for the Public Schools, 2 West 45th Street, New York 19, New York.

If the citizens committee is to achieve maximum effectiveness it will be necessary for it to begin with a list of specific problems on which some sort of agreement is desirable. It will attempt also to make a distinction between those professional decisions best left to the teacher and those policy matters appropriately decided upon by the committee.

One group of committees has suggested that "nothing is so sacred that it can't be studied by a citizens committee which is genuinely working for the welfare of the children and economy." While it may be true that the committee has a right to study even professional problems, it seems reasonable to question the wisdom of their doing so. It seems unlikely that a citizens committee for the public hospitals would or should take unto itself the responsibility for advising the physicians as to methods of treatment.

The educational problems which are most specifically professional are those having to do with methods of instruction
including the planning and organization of instruction. Decisions regarding these matters are dependent upon a large body
of rather technical information regarding the nature of the
learning process and the nature of the learner. The teacher has,
or ought to have, a much better grasp of this information than
can reasonably be expected of those who are not professional
teachers.

The problem of textbook selection is closely related to that
of instructional methods. In a catechismal school, in which
orthodoxy is the aim, the textbook or catechism is all important,
and the teacher is of relatively minor importance. The textbook is presumed to contain the truth, and only the truth is
presented to the child in order that he may not be confused.
But the textbook used in the public school is not a catechism.
It is an instrument of instruction and can be properly judged
only in terms of its relationship to instructional methods. Passages may not properly be judged out of context nor can the
entire book be judged out of the context of the classroom procedures in which it is used. Its selection is therefore a very
complex professional problem.

In cities in which widespread controversy over textbooks has
developed, it may be wise for the teachers to discuss their textbooks with the citizens. They can explain how the textbook is
used and how it is interpreted. The citizens may occasionally
be able to point out bits of propaganda or misinformation
which the teacher has overlooked. Certainly textbooks have
sometimes been biased and have sometimes contained outright
examples of error, and the teacher should surely be aware of
such bias and such error. But if textbooks were selected by
someone other than professional teachers, it seems likely that

errors and biases would still creep in occasionally, and a text-book so selected would be much more difficult for the teacher to coordinate with his instructional methods. A textbook so selected might be virtually unteachable when used by the age group for whom it is selected, or it might duplicate other books which the child has already studied.

Another difficulty is that most of the books used in secondary and higher education are not *textbooks* at all, and there has been a tendency in some schools to discard textbooks altogether. This tendency is endorsed, for different reasons, by educators representing such very divergent points of view as those of the extreme progressives, on the one hand, and the Great Books people on the other.

A course in literature may include the reading of selections from a wide variety of writers including Milton, Shakespeare, Dickens, Poe, Thoreau, and Sinclair Lewis. Surely there is no implication that the teacher who selects the writings of these authors fully accepts the views of any of them or that such acceptance is expected of the student. Dickens, it is charged, is anti-Semitic; Shakespeare believes in ghosts; Thoreau approves of civil insurrection; and Lewis takes a dim view of the Rotary Club. If the books read in a literature course must be acceptable in all details to all citizens, there is very little literature which is likely to pass muster. The class may be reduced to reading *Elsie Dinsmore*. The important thing is the total effect of the literature course on the student, and the teacher who works with students year after year ought to be able to judge this better than can those more distantly removed from the classroom.

A mature student who is to gain some understanding of international politics may properly be asked to read the works of Plato, Nietzsche, and Marx despite the fact that all of these writers proposed political systems totally unacceptable to our way of thinking. Without a thorough understanding of nazism, fascism, monarchy, and of communism, he may fail to recognize these forms of government when they appear under other names. Of course the intelligent and informed citizen understands this and may properly examine all the books which students are asked to read, but a citizens committee which attempts to censor the school books is likely to do more harm than good to the cause of democratic education.

There remain a number of very important problems of school policy which can very profitably be discussed by the citizens committee. These may be summarized as follows:

I. What are the fundamental aims or purposes of the public school? Under this major heading come several important specific questions.
   1. What part of the cultural heritage should be passed on to all children by the schools?
   2. To what extent is the school responsible for character education?
   3. To what extent is the school responsible for supervising the child's recreation?
   4. To what extent is vocational training the job of the schools?
   5. Under our Constitution and our laws what part, if any, can or should the school play in the religious life of the child? To what extent should it contribute to his knowledge and understanding of the various religions?
   6. How important is athletics?

II. What are the fundamental skills? How much skill in mathematics, reading, and in oral and written use of our language is fundamental? Is a knowledge of foreign languages essential?

III. At what age should the child enter school? There exists a remarkable uniformity in the choice of the age of six, but little logic lies behind this choice. Perhaps the child should enter

school at four or at eight. Perhaps the decision should be based upon factors quite apart from chronological age.

IV. Through what ages should school attendance be compulsory?

V. For what period of the child's life should the public provide the financial support for his education? Should junior colleges become a part of universal public education? Should opportunities for adult education be provided at public expense?

VI. What type of reports should be made to the parents regarding the child's school progress?

Teachers and educators have already given much thought to all of these problems and they can provide the citizens groups with much information that will be useful to them. But the final decisions are for the people.

When the first citizens groups were established teachers felt some apprehension lest these groups infringe upon purely professional matters of a kind best left to the teachers. But in many communities such fears have been allayed, and teachers and school administrators have come to welcome the citizens committees and to turn to them for guidance and assistance when the schools are attacked by pressure groups less representative of all the people. In its best development the citizens committee is an excellent example of democracy at work. It offers an effective method of reconciling some of the conflicts and of bringing the schools back to the people.

# CHAPTER XV

# THE FUNDAMENTAL ISSUE

In my preface I took the position that this was to be not a book of answers but a book of information for those who wish to draw their own conclusions. Maintaining this position has not proved easy. One who has struggled for twenty years and more with the problems of education quite naturally has reached some conclusions, formed some opinions, acquired some prejudices; inevitably these influence the selection of materials and the treatment of ideas.

In a controversy the one who chooses an intermediate position is beset by difficulties not encountered by the extremist. The extremist has his back (or is it his face?) to the wall and so can be attacked from only one side. The moderate stands in the center of the arena and is vulnerable from all angles. In the field of education there are many who try to find the golden mean, but few of these write books because once the book appears in print the moderate is likely to find himself driven up against one or another of the walls, and thus he ceases to be moderate. Another difficulty is that a moderate book does not sell well and therefore often is not welcomed by the publisher.

There is a danger, too, that the moderate will seem to avoid taking a firm position on the fundamental issues and that he will give the appearance of being uncertain. It is dramatic to describe an object as pitch black or snow white; no one is excited by the suggestion that it is really a middling gray, and one who so describes it will be accused of being unable to make up his mind. But it so happens that some things *are* middling gray. One of these things is public education in the United States as of 1953.

Our thinking about education is in a state of confusion but the schools themselves are neither so bad as some critics have said nor so good as our publicity agents make them appear. The worst thing about contemporary education is its confused philosophy which is reflected in the educational journals and in some of the textbooks of education. Any well-educated person who reads these garbled interpretations of pragmatic philosophy is likely to conclude that education has become the antithesis of clear thinking.

The best thing about contemporary education is that a great many classroom teachers ignore the gobbledygook and the pedaguese and go right ahead and do a sensible job of teaching. If one visits the classrooms instead of reading the journals, he may well conclude that the schools are not so bad after all. It depends on which classroom you visit; but I for one, if I again had to face the prospect of twelve years as a pupil in a public school, would far rather take my chances in a school of today than return to the schools I attended between 1913 and 1925. The schools I attended had none of the characteristics commonly attributed to the schools of an earlier day. There was little memorization and drill, and we did not learn many facts. Yet the schools I attended were certainly not "progressive"; it was just that the teachers were unprepared for their jobs both in intellect and in education. Of the twenty or so teachers

I encountered in elementary and high school, three or four were really competent and, fortunately, two of them were superb.

The child starting to school today has a good chance of encountering a much larger number of competent teachers, and the worst that he meets will surely be no worse than those of a generation ago. Most of his teachers will have a better understanding of children and of the fact that children are very different from one another. Not all of his teachers will be liberally educated, but the proportion who are will be much higher than was true a generation ago, particularly among the teachers of the lower grades. And more of his teachers will be professional in the sense that they plan to make a career of teaching.

The child will probably study in a building which is better heated and ventilated, where the light is not so hard on the eyes, and in which the seats are more comfortable. These things are not the essence of education but they help to make the school a pleasant place in which to work. Yet there is more than an outside chance that the child will attend school in the same old firetrap of a building which was attended by his parents. The worst of our school buildings are a good deal less habitable than are the factories and offices in which the father spends his day or the home in which the mother spends hers. Our willingness to house children in some of these buildings is little short of a national scandal.

Another risk run by today's child is that there will be far too many children in his class to allow for effective teaching. A teacher who can do a superb job with twenty or twenty-five children becomes little more than a custodian and a policeman when the class size is increased to forty. Teachers are not responsible for the increased birth rate, but the parents are and they must accept the responsibility for seeing that there are enough classrooms and enough teachers. As of 1953 there are not nearly enough of either.

Despite all these problems, and despite their difficult position in being caught between the attacks of the critics and the pressures of the frontier thinkers in education, many teachers are doing reasonably well at a most difficult job.

But the schools of 1960 and of 1970 ought to do a much better job than is being done today. I think there is a fair chance that they will if we do two things: First, we must find more good potential teachers, educate them better, and pay them well enough to keep them from leaving the profession. Second, we must decide just what we want the schools to accomplish—we must clarify our educational philosophy.

Finding better teachers and preparing them more adequately is in part the responsibility of the teachers colleges, but the type of preparation will be dependent upon our decisions about what is to be expected of the schools. These decisions have not been made and it is this lack of decision which has led to the contemporary confusion in education.

Though the people must decide, it is appropriate that professional educators should propose. But for twenty years or more the educators have merely reiterated the same set of proposals in various guises, the proposals which have centered around that vague ideology known as "progressive education." If these proposals had been acceptable to the public and found workable by the classroom teachers all would be well. But neither group has been satisfied. As a reform movement progressive education played its useful part, but as a clear and workable philosophy it has been found wanting. It is too vague, too emotional, too anti-intellectual to be acceptable to the majority. It has failed to tell us what is more important and what is less important in education, and this is the essential function of an educational philosophy.

It is not the purpose of the present book to propose the new philosophy of education, but I hope that I have clarified some of the issues and have cleared away some of the cobwebs.

II

The fundamental issue in education today is not whether something called "progressive education" is better than some other kind of education. Nor is the issue between the education of 1953 and the education of one generation or a hundred generations ago. The question facing us is this: What is good education for American children?

Readers who are less familiar with the ideas of Dewey than with those of his interpreters may be surprised to learn that the above paragraph is a reasonably accurate paraphrase of the last two pages of *Experience and Education*. We shall learn what we can from the past, but let us prepare for the future. What we must decide upon today is the course of education for the coming years. We must ask ourselves what education will best prepare the children who are now in the schools to be adults in the tumultuous years ahead. We must look into the best crystal ball available. We must predict, we must estimate, we must—if necessary—guess.

One important prediction seems reasonably safe. The coming half century will continue to be a period of rapid change. However obvious this may seem, it is a prediction of greatest importance to education. In the histories of all the great civilizations may be found periods, often centuries in length, during which time has seemed to stand still, periods in which decade followed decade with so little change that an education for the recent past might serve very well as a preparation for the probable future. We live in no such period. In a period of change, sound education must include a thorough grounding in those things which, while least likely to change themselves, are necessary in preparation for change. What are those things?

Even in such apparently practical areas as vocational training the best training for a period of change is not that which is most specific or most immediately useful. A course of study in automobile mechanics which ignores theory and broad general principles, which teaches the student exactly how to repair a car of 1953 vintage, which enables him to learn all the specific skills involved in adjusting a carburetor, in grinding valves, and in repairing a transmission may prove utterly useless to him before he reaches the age of forty. It is entirely possible that the automobile of 1973 will have no carburetor, no valves, and no transmission recognizable to the mechanic of the present day. This student will, in 1973, find himself well trained in the repairing of a vehicle which will have become as rare as is the Model T today and which may differ from the car of 1953 far more than that car differs from the Model T. The mechanic who knows only specifics of the "how to do it" variety will find it difficult indeed to keep up with the change.

But this by no means indicates that the schools cannot prepare the auto mechanic for his job in 1973 or even in the year 2000. For there are many things which he needs to know, things closely related to his job which will not change. The laws of mechanics will not be repealed, nor will the principles of electricity. The principle of the lever will be the same in 1990 as it is today, as will the facts of the conductivity of metals and of electromagnetics. A solid, well-taught course in physics will be of lasting value long after a course in engine repair has become archaic. The emphasis must be on *well* taught. The course in physics must be so presented that the student understands the relation of the principles of physics to the self-propelling vehicles of today and tomorrow.

In the long run, as Dewey has so well pointed out, theory is the most practical of all things; it is the most practical because it has the widest applications. It is unfortunate that the extremists in progressive education have ignored this fact. In their enthusiasm for the immediately useful they have sometimes maintained that a world of change is one in which there are no stable facts worth teaching.

The astrophysicist, concerning himself with the mechanics of this and other universes, has been forced to admit that Newtonian physics is not quite so absolute as it once appeared—in the vast distances of the galaxies even light does not follow straight paths. But for those of us who live on the surface of this tiny planet the laws of mechanics which have served so well for the past two or three centuries will continue to be stable and useful facts for the mechanic of the coming years. Light will continue, for all his purposes, to follow straight lines. Friction will continue to increase temperatures, and metals, when heated, will continue to expand. Magnetic forces will operate much as they always have, and the laws of inertia will remain in effect. There is no dearth of stable facts which the mechanic can profitably learn.

But the mechanic is much more than a mechanic. He is a member of a family group, he will probably be a husband and a father, he will surely be a citizen, a citizen in a democracy who has both rights and obligations. What can the school teach to prepare him for these obligations? We can and should teach reading better than it has ever been taught. We can teach the child to read rapidly and with understanding, to differentiate between fact and opinion, and to judge the significance of that which he reads. We can teach him to use simple arithmetic more easily and more rapidly and to understand the significance of his computations. All but the least able children can learn these things well before they reach the high school. While learning these skills they can learn a great deal about the world and about man's past. Whether we call this history and geography, or combine the two into the social studies, the ideas involved should be learned thoroughly and the parts should be put together. A few random units or projects will not do, for such study leaves too many gaps. It is not enough that a child does a project on the Eskimos, one on the Romans, one on the Indians, and one on the Chinese. There is never time for enough such units to cover the necessary ground. The child must know something of the whole world and must come to see it whole. But to understand the whole he must know something of all the parts. Geography as a setting for history is probably the most neglected subject in the schools today, but never has such knowledge been needed so badly. We are sending boys to Korea to fight who never heard of Korea during their school years. Is it any wonder that they do not understand its importance?

In the high school the student should gain a thorough understanding of federal, state, and local governments, and of the difference between our government and the government of other nations. The Constitution of the United States will continue to be altered through the years by amendments and by new interpretations, but every student should have a thorough understanding of the original document; without such knowledge he will be unprepared for his role as an adult citizen.

The principles of sociology, psychology, and political science are no less important than are those of the physical sciences; indeed, they are more important to us because they deal more directly with mankind. Unfortunately they are less perfectly known and, at present, much less certainly predictive. This is true not because the sociologist, the psychologist, or the political scientist is less competent than is the physicist but because the variables are far more numerous. Even so there is a considerable and growing body of reasonably firm knowledge about social organization, the origins of prejudice, the nature and extent of individual differences, the nature of personal and social conflict, and such information should be made available to the high-school student. In all of these fields there is a great deal of factual knowledge which every citizen will need. These are, if you like, mere facts, but as Superintendent Spinning asked in his annual address to the teachers of Rochester, "What is so mere about a fact?" Facts are essential; sound judgments cannot be made without them. Let no one tell us that in an age of pragmatism there are no facts sufficiently stable to be worth teaching or that facts are unimportant.

But our education for the future need not be and should not be limited to facts. Our judgments as to what is most important in literature will alter somewhat with the passing years, but the great literature of the past will continue to give stability and continuity to our values and meaning to our lives. New tastes in music and art will develop, but the child who has an understanding of the music and art of the past will be better prepared to understand the new. The great problems of philosophy will still be with us, but in such realms of philosophy as ethics, where daily decisions must be made, the child who learns something of the solutions which have been proposed during the past millennia will be best prepared to make at least tentative conclusions to guide his course of action.

The struggle for human freedom will continue, and freedom will continue to be fundamental. New dogmas will replace pragmatism as pragmatism has replaced the dogmas of the past, and the student must learn that these new dogmas can, if un-questioned, become as stultifying as were the dogmas of other years. New dictators, or would-be dictators, will continue to attempt to gain control over free men, and the student must come to understand the corrupting effect of unlimited power over human beings. He must understand that a tyrant, what-ever names he may assume, however much he professes to do his deeds in the interests of humanity, must in the long run destroy those things which free men hold most dear.

There is no dearth of facts, of principles, or higher truths for us to teach and to learn. Let us get on with the learning and the teaching. Let us demand and get better teachers. Let us make teaching so attractive and so honored a calling that the best and most able of our youth will knock at the doors and demand admission. Let us make the teachers colleges the very best colleges in the nation, at least the equivalent of the very best liberal arts colleges and the very best medical schools. And to these colleges for teachers let us attract the very best of our young men and young women—not the leftovers from the other professions.

If as a people, we really understand the importance of education in a democracy, this can and shall be done.

# RELATED READING

I list below some useful books for those interested in the public schools and in the contemporary controversy in education. I have endeavored to select books representing a variety of points of view, and have appended my own critical comments.

—P. W.

Barzun, Jacques, *Teacher in America*, Little, Brown & Company, Boston, 1945.

In his opening sentence Barzun states flatly, "Education is indeed the dullest of subjects and I intend to say as little about it as I can." Mr. Barzun then proceeds to talk very entertainingly about practically nothing else for 300 pages.

Barzun's comments are worth reading as the observations of an intelligent European who has been in America long enough to have drawn some conclusions about American education, conclusions which are often very perceptive. The reader should be warned that the term "teacher" as used in this book means college or university teacher, and that the author shows little knowledge of or interest in the public schools. Even at the college level his knowledge is largely limited to Columbia University and specifically to Columbia College which he says is highly representative of modern instruction throughout the country.

Bell, Bernard Iddings, *Crisis in Education: A Challenge to American Complacency*, McGraw-Hill Book Company, Inc., New York, 1949.

Canon Bell of the Protestant Episcopal Church has long been critical of the contemporary trend toward relativism, secularism, and egalitarianism. He holds that the public school must accept much of the blame for this trend and in stating his thesis has been one of the most vigorous critics of the schools. He differs from some of the harsh critics in that no one can question his integrity or his sincerity.

While many will agree with some of Dr. Bell's criticisms, it does not seem likely that his own philosophy of education can be accepted by a majority of Americans. He holds that the business of education is to minister to the common need and that "the common need is for reverence toward That Which Is and for discipline in the light of what such reverence reveals" (p. 178).

This philosophy of education is an outgrowth of Dr. Bell's own theological and philosophical convictions as is his contention that the public schools should do much more than is now done to promote religion. If the public schools will not teach religion, Dr. Bell thinks that the state should give financial support to private schools. The constitutional objections to these proposals are waved aside rather lightly.

Those who consider it essential to maintain the separation of church and state, those who do not share Canon Bell's fear of secularism, may still profitably read this book as an excellent statement of a point of view which needs to be understood by those responsible for the school. All readers will be interested in the specific recommendations contained in the last chapter, "First Steps in Reformation." Several of these proposals may be acceptable to those who are looking for a middle road in education.

Bode, Boyd H., *Progressive Education at the Crossroads*, Newson & Company, New York, 1938.

This little book of only 128 pages is perhaps the best critical examination of progressive education to be found anywhere. Though Bode himself has usually been classified as a progressive educator, he has always steered cleared of the lunatic fringes, and his tone is calm and reasonable. Unlike many of the progressives, he has never hesitated to criticize the movement of which he is a part. He is exceptional also in his clear understanding of philosophies other than his own and in the care which he takes to avoid allowing his opinions to petrify into dogmas.

James B. Conant, *Education and Liberty*, Harvard University Press, 1953.

This book is based upon a series of lectures which Dr. Conant, who was then president of Harvard, delivered at the University of Virginia in February, 1952. Conant's inquiry is focused on the education of the adolescent between the ages of twelve and twenty, and his problem is that of determining how best to provide instruction to this age group in a modern democracy, a problem which will be intensified by the increase in school population which faces us as a result of the rise in birth rate.

The first of the three chapters presents a comparison of British and American education. The second chapter considers the four-year liberal arts college in the United States and its influence on secondary or high-school education, and the third outlines some of the problems we now face in the United States and suggests possible answers. Nearly half of the book consists of notes which include a great deal of statistical material which will be useful to those who are planning for the education of tomorrow.

It is Conant's view that the doctrine of equality in the United States has come to mean "not parity of status for all adults but equality of opportunity for the young." In this Conant is in agreement with Thomas Jefferson whose views on education and interest in securing true democracy he shares.

Conant's solutions do not include extending the present type of college education to all high-school graduates. He would, on the contrary, restrict education in the four-year college and the university to students of conspicuous ability. For the less able he would provide an expanded two-year college course, and he would make these lower-level colleges more fashionable by awarding a bachelor's degree to their graduates. Such a solution would make it possible for the four-year colleges to hold to high academic standards for the more able students without denying all higher education to the less able. It would make it possible to "combine the British concern for training the 'natural aristocracy of talents' with the American insistence on general education for all future citizens."

Counts, George S., *Education and American Civilization*, Columbia
    University Press, New York, 1952.

Twenty years ago Counts was one of the group of educators who
urged that the democratic tradition should be transferred from
individualistic to collectivist economic foundations. Many readers
interpreted this as an encouragement for a trend toward communism.

In this book Counts makes it very clear that he vigorously and
energetically opposes any development of communism in America.
He considers Russian communism both profoundly reactionary and
imperialistic. His opinion is important because Counts knows much
more about the recent developments in Russia than do most American educators, having lived in that country and having studied the
Russian schools at first hand.

Counts remains a controversial figure in education, but this book
can profitably be read as an intelligent analysis of the relation between education and democracy.

Cunningham, William F., *The Pivotal Problems of Education*, The
    Macmillan Company, New York, 1940.

This book, by a professor of education at the University of Notre
Dame, is a reasonably balanced presentation of the leading contemporary philosophies of education. The author's own point of
view, which he clearly states, is consistent with that of the Roman
Catholic Church. He chooses to call this "supernaturalism."

The book provides valuable background material, not only for
those who share Dr. Cunningham's religious convictions but to
others who wish to understand the point of view taken by his
church on educational matters. However, the implied identification
of idealism with fascism and the classification of pragmatism as a
subbranch of materialism will be unacceptable to a great many
readers.

Dewey, John, *Experience and Education*, The Macmillan Company,
    New York, 1939.

This is probably the most readable of Dewey's books and one that
should be read with care by all who wish to see the difference

between Dewey's own ideas on education and the ideas of those who profess to be his followers.

Writing in 1938, after he had had an opportunity to see the extent to which his own ideas had been distorted, Dewey finds it necessary to call attention to the dangerous tendency of pragmatism to become dogmatic. While holding to his own basic tenets, he makes it clear that he never believed that all experiences are genuinely or equally educative or that experience and education can be directly equated to each other. Some experiences, he emphasizes, are mis-educative.

While denying that facts are the ends of education, he wants it clearly understood that facts are important means toward ends. He has no wish to eliminate the teaching of facts; he wishes only to keep them in their proper perspective. He does not wish to eliminate discipline; he wishes only to move gradually toward self-discipline.

If this book were unsigned, many readers would say that the writer was not a progressive but a moderate individual taking a position midway between progressivism and the better aspects of traditional education.

*General Education in a Free Society*, Report of the Harvard Committee, Harvard University Press, Cambridge, Mass., 1945.

In the spring of 1943 President Conant of Harvard appointed a University Committee on the Objectives of a General Education in a Free Society, with members drawn from the faculties of Arts and Sciences and of Education. In his instructions to the committee, he urged them to consider the problem of general education in both the school and the college. He cautioned the committee that the general education of the great majority of each generation in the high schools is vastly more important than that of the comparatively small minority who attend four-year colleges. He suggested that the educational process falls short of its ideal unless it includes at each stage of maturity some continuing contact with liberal and humane studies.

This book is the published report of the work of the Harvard Committee and has come to be referred to among educators as the Harvard Report. It represents an exhaustive study of secondary and collegiate education, deals briefly with the history of American education, gives a good deal of attention to the theory of general education, and considers the relation of each of the major areas of knowledge to the problems of general education. The conclusions reached by this committee should be considered by all who are concerned with educational policy.

Kilpatrick, William Heard, *Philosophy of Education*, The Macmillan Company, New York, 1951.

Kilpatrick, "The Million Dollar Professor" of Columbia's Teachers College, has long been the leading apostle of the new education. This book, written near the end of his long career, is a statement of the conclusions which he has reached, a summary of his own educational philosophy.

Though this book is used as a textbook in courses called "Philosophy of Education," the title of the book is misleading. This is not so much an inquiry into first principles as a statement of those principles accepted by Kilpatrick—and now accepted by a great many educators—with a development of the ideas and practices which result from the acceptance of those principles. Other philosophies are introduced only as a foil for Kilpatrick's views and are not presented in a way which would be acceptable to his opponents. This book should be read by all who wish to understand the "new" point of view in education. But one who wishes to evaluate contemporary trends in their proper perspective will find it necessary to read the works of those who differ with Kilpatrick. The student of education who gets all his philosophy from this volume will conclude that other points of view are so reactionary, so unenlightened, or so uninformed as to be deserving of no consideration whatever.

Knight, Edgar W., *Fifty Years of American Education*, The Ronald Press Company, New York, 1952.

This is a historical review and a critical appraisal of education during the past fifty years. The author, who is Kenan Professor of Educational History at the University of North Carolina, is well informed and free of bias. For the period which it covers this is probably the best of the many histories of education.

Rugg, Harold, and B. Marian Brooks, *The Teacher in School and Society*, World Book Company, Yonkers, N. Y., 1950.

This is a textbook used in teachers colleges as a basis for the course which introduces the prospective teacher to his profession. The name of the senior author will be widely recognized by those who have given attention to the current educational controversy because Dr. Rugg's high-school textbooks have been criticized in many places as "socialistic" or worse. Citizens who wish to judge Rugg's point of view for themselves may profitably read this book.

Smith, Mortimer, *And Madly Teach*, Henry Regnery Company, Chicago, 1949.

This little book of only 107 pages is one of the most intelligent and effective of the many recent documents attacking the philosophy and the doctrines which underlie modern education. Mr. Smith's point of view is that of a citizen who became concerned over contemporary trends when he became a member of a school board and who took the trouble to inform himself regarding the philosophies as well as the practices of the schools. Unlike some of our critics, he has a pretty thorough understanding of the philosophy of pragmatism and of its applications in education—a better understanding than is possessed by many members of the teaching profession.

Mr. Smith's criticisms are really rather devastating. That they have not been answered by the educators seems to indicate either that the educators have no adequate answers or that they do not recognize the difference between effective criticism and that which is so "crackpot" as to be undeserving of a reply.

# About the Author

Paul Woodring was born in Delta, Ohio, on July 16, 1907. He attended rural and village schools and entered Bowling Green University where he enrolled as a pre-law student. But two years of college depleted his funds, and he got a job as a country schoolteacher in Rocky Ridge, Ohio, at $1044 a year. The following year he taught in a junior high school in Maumee after which he returned to Bowling Green where he received his bachelor's degree in education in 1930.

For three years Mr. Woodring taught literature in a senior high school at Rossford, a suburb of Toledo, and spent his summers hitchhiking through the West, working in national forests and in the harvest fields. In 1933 he went to Ohio State University where he took his master's degree in psychology, following which he lived for two years in Los Angeles, attending evening courses at the University of Southern California while working at a variety of short jobs including one which involved a study of the educational programs in the CCC camps of California.

In 1935 he returned to Ohio State as a part-time instructor and received his doctor of philosophy degree from that institution in 1938. After two years as a clinical psychologist for the Detroit Criminal Courts he moved in 1939 to Western Washington College in Bellingham, Washington, where he is now a professor of psychology and teaches courses in psychology, education, and philosophy. With his wife he lives in a modern house which they designed and built themselves.

Professor Woodring entered the Army in 1942 as a first lieutenant, serving two years as a personnel officer at various posts in the United States, and subsequently going overseas as an information and education officer on General MacArthur's staff in Australia, New Guinea, Manila, and Tokyo. After serving as commandant of the Armed Forces Institute, Western Pacific Branch, he was discharged in 1946 with the rank of lieutenant colonel.